Journey
Solitude

Ann Petre

First Published in 2006 by Milton Contact Ltd.
www.miltoncontact.com
in co-operation with *Moyhill* Publishing

A CIP catalogue record for this book is available from the British Library.

ISBN 1-905597-04-5
ISBN 978-1-905597-04-8

Designed & typeset by *Moyhill* Publishing
Cover photographs by Hugh Hales-Tooke

Printed in UK

Book Sales in Ireland and UK
Moyhill Publishing,
12 Eaton Brae, Shankill, Co. Dublin, Ireland.

Book Sales in continental Europe
Moyhill Publishing,
Avenida Sicilia 54, 28420 Galapagar, Madrid, Spain.

Order online at *http://www.moyhill.com*
or **e-mail** *orders@moyhill.com*

Autobiographical Notes

Ann Hales-Tooke, nee Petre

The author gained an Oxford degree in Modern Greats in 1947. After various administrative jobs, work in an agricultural firm near Cambridge led to her marriage and to her raising three sons there. Interest in early child development and freelance writing led to her involvement with the movement to liberalise the care of children in hospital. She wrote two books about this and became a Governor of the United Cambridge Hospitals in 1970.

In 1977, after gaining a P.G.C.E. (Postgraduate Certificate in Education), she worked in primary and special schools specialising in the teaching of sign language. For this she was awarded a Research Associateship at the then Institute of Education in 1984. She trained as a psychodynamic counsellor with the Cambridgeshire Consultancy in Counselling. She gained BACP (British Association for Counselling and Psychotherapy) accreditation and taught counselling for a number of years for the university.

Recently she has travelled to many Bronze Age sites to make paintings of ancient sacred places. She has exhibited at the Tavistock Foundation and with the Cambridge Open Studios for the past twelve years.

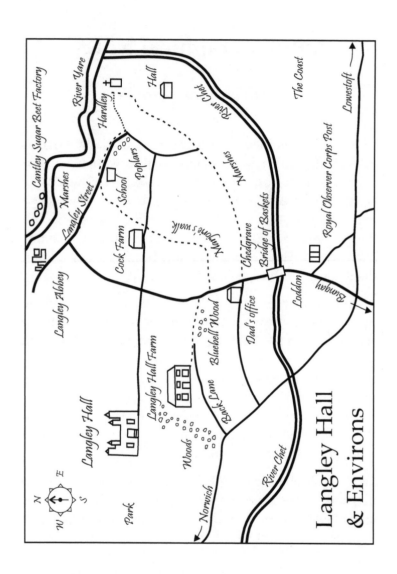

Langley Hall
& Environs

For My Parents

Contents

Contents

List of Photographs & illustrations

List of Photographs & illustrations

Foreword

This is emphatically *not a family history*. Nor, strictly speaking, a memoir.

It is more a story, or a myth. It is a narrative woven round my life. It attempts to explain why people, including myself, behaved as they did. It looks for the motives of our actions, the influences we have had upon each other, the origins of our behaviour.

Sometimes, instead of facts, I have used my imagination. The story lies, as stories do, somewhere between fact and fiction. Some names and events have been changed.

I wanted to illustrate the different decades of the twentieth century as I have lived through them. What is going on around us in society and politics affects our personal lives profoundly. I recount my particularly painful experience of living through the times of Women's Lib in the sixties and seventies. To live as a white, middle class, English woman in 2006 is light years away from the living our mother experienced from 1902–1982.

Looking back, the view changes all the time. What I feel today about myself, my parents, the other people in my life has changed very much from what I felt even a decade ago. I am sure it will change again. This story is about how it looks to me today on my 80th birthday, March 27th, 2006.

Ann Hales-Tooke (nee Petre)

Prologue

The Abbey House

The house was home to a number of people – both living and dead.

It was an unusual house. Unexpected. Most who daily hurried past its high garden walls, and the pollarded limes that towered above them, spared no thought for what lay within. Perhaps the house wanted to be forgotten. Certainly it stood on ground that was both holy and unholy.

Did I grow too interested in the Abbey House? Was I obsessed by it? I lived near it for decades and had to paint it frequently.

The house was built of small dark red Dutch bricks. It looked like a house in a painting by Pieter de Hoogh, but its foundations were much older, laid with stone from the mediaeval priory that stood there from 1112 until it was destroyed on the orders of Henry VIII in 1536.

It was not a cheerful house. Locals said that babies born there never settled. People lived uneasily within its walls. If they left they failed to find happiness. People who stayed on in the house longed to get away.

Last Christmas there was a full moon, also snow – several inches. The owners of the house were away but I

1

had their permission to paint there when I liked. As I am old, I wrapped up warmly and sat with my easel near the great lancet window that illumined the staircase leading to the ballroom. I wanted to catch the shadows cast by the towering chimneys.

Suddenly there were lights in the driveway. The main gates that had been chained and padlocked swung open. Without a sound, a procession of monks came through the gates and moved along the drive towards the front door. As I watched, the walls of the house melted away and in their place slowly arose the shadowy outlines of a great mediaeval church. First the West End with carvings round the doorway, then the Nave and the Transepts and finally a lantern Tower grew out of the crossing. A bell began to toll as the monks led by a server carrying a cross went over the threshold into the church.

Instinctively I began to paint what I was seeing. Thick snowflakes started to float down but did not settle on the black habits of the monks or the vestments of the Abbot robed for Midnight Mass. As the procession disappeared into the church I noticed there were no footprints in the snow on the drive. The gates swung shut and distant voices from the church intoned 'Kyrie Eleison...Christe Eleison." Mass was starting.

Very slowly the lancet windows started to glow, as if candles had been lit within. I heard the organ and voices singing the familiar plain-chant of my school days. I wanted to go in. The music got louder. I felt intensely cold. The next thing I remember, I was not in church but back at the very beginning...

I

Early Days

The 1920s

It's March 1st, 1926. "Which way today?" Marjorie asked as she walked away from the house down the drive. The March wind was strong but not as biting as last week. Huge white clouds pushed impatiently against each other as they headed south east. Deep purple shadows were cast by one cloud on another. She noticed that as they jostled for space, up there, patches of bright blue appeared in the cotton wool. She decided to do the six mile round. In Snow's Lane there were no buds yet on the oak trees, but the solitary ash was beginning to show green. "If the Ash is out before the Oak, oh! baby mine, this summer we shall have a soak. Baby George kicked hard in response. (My mother a loving but not overly imaginative woman, has given no thought to the possibility that I am a girl. William wants a son so he can teach him to farm.)

Cock Farm, also called Boundary Farm, red brick with a pantile roof, came into sight across the field on her left. At the crossroads she waited while a horseman guided his plough, pulled by two Suffolk Punches, across the road into the field. Then she set off briskly down Gentleman's Walk towards Langley Street. Despite her considerable girth, she strode along energetically. I loved the rhythm of her walking, first down into a small valley and then up an incline. Next, a long walk downhill into Langley Street. By now the view had opened out. She was able to see two miles across the marshes to Cantley Sugar Beet Factory, belching out white smoke and an all-pervading smell of burnt sugar, on the far side of the river Yare. Cattle grazed on marshes shaped by geometrical dykes. The sails of Hardley drainage mill turned furiously in the wind.

We reached the Street and turned right beside the village school. Could I hear the shouts of the children out at play? My mother paused to have a word with the teacher in the playground?

"We were hoping Mrs Peters (they always got the name slightly wrong) that you might like to come with Mrs Beauchamp to the children's Easter Play if Baby (She glanced downwards) hasn't come by March 30th?"

My mother accepted the invitation; it was nice to be asked. She was a bit muddled about her due date. A diary entry suggests she half expected George on April 23rd – hence the choice of name perhaps?

She walked on along the Street, past several large farms with manure filled cow yards emitting a rich odour. It was an interesting lane dividing two different terrains, rather like a coast road. On her right were rolling arable fields, pale green with winter sown corn, on her left an expanse of marsh crisscrossed by water.

There were no roads across the marshes. It was a long journey to reach the villages on the other side of the river. Marjorie felt cut off from the rest of the world by an inland sea of grass.

For some reason this bit of the road always depressed her. She was lonely. She missed the hills of her native Salop and the local people with their lilting half Welsh intonation. She missed her dominant mother who always had the answer. She missed her father's teasing. She missed her chickens and goats and her Welsh cob Lucy.

What had she expected when she had married William the previous June? She had not realised how preoccupied he would be with work. He was out all day and when he came home he would pour himself a large pink gin and begin a long session of business calls.

Before dinner he always bathed and changed into a dinner jacket. At the meal, which was at least three courses, they were waited on by Minnie, the house parlour maid, in her lace cap and frilly apron. Perhaps its formality frightened Marjorie. She certainly told me, often, that she felt her chatter about the day's events might seem trivial to her husband. He was a serious and a well read man, and fourteen years her senior. He enjoyed company. If she invited his friends to dinner he was a genial host but she found this crowd rather daunting as they were all considerably older than her. If they played bridge she felt she always played badly. William's obvious liking for the wife of one couple made Marjorie uneasy. There were many things about his long bachelor life that she knew nothing about.

These things she told me, many times, down the years. But I feel I sort of knew them, in shadowy outline, from those months in the womb, and from those long, solitary walks. I grew up her confidant, her soul mate, her best friend, and later, her protector.

The poignancy of those days was only one of the many emotions we shared.

More important was the unspeakable joy. I was loved and cherished and I was coming into being.

Her mood lightened as we approached a double line of poplar trees.

They reminded her of pictures she'd seen of France. She loved paintings and Mrs Beauchamp –Aunt Sheila– William's employer and owner of the Langley estate, had lent her a book of the Impressionist painters. These Langley poplars are just like ones in some of Monet's paintings. William doesn't like these painters. He hates the way they daub on the paint. This surprised my mother who thinks they paint like Constable, whom my father admired. Now my mother thinks of her best friend from school, Sibella, always called Aunt Sib. She'd just married Joy, an artist who admired the Impressionists. They've gone to live near Monte Carlo. They have very little money –his paintings weren't selling– but she sounds very happy in her letters. Their first baby is due soon.

By this time we had reached the top of the hill by Hardley Church. From here Marjorie could see right across the Hardley and the Chedgrave marshes. She could see the sails of yachts below the river banks and the place where the river Chet ran into the Yare. She looks down the hill to Hardley Hall, a grey stone Tudor farmhouse that is said to be haunted. William says that's as may be but no tenant stays very long. She shivers. It looks very isolated there, right on the edge of the marsh and no other houses near by.

She was beginning to feel tired so she sat down in a sheltered corner of the graveyard. Here out of the wind the spring sun was warm on her face. A blackbird was singing. She bent to smell a clump of early primroses. Suddenly we were shot through by an ecstatic sense of happiness. We were wildly in love with life, the world, my father and each other.

My mother and I did not get to see the Langley children's play, I arrived on March 27th and I was to be Ann...

Langley Hall Farm

After eighty years I can close my eyes and "see" the house from the bottom of the drive by the iron gate that was always hooked open. Lately I found its stone gatepost tumbled into the long grass. The ground, on the right, drops away to a large field, now named "Petre's Field" in honour of our father. On the left is a wood of sycamores. It is marked on the ordinance survey as the 'Common Plantation', but we have always called it the Bluebell Wood because of its sheet of blue flowers in April. As the sun warmed the flowers the scent was like no other – fresh honey that did not cloy. Opposite the wood my father planted a thousand daffodils that bloom every March.

The drive curved slightly to the left. On the right was a line of ten gigantic sweet chestnut trees, planted centuries ago. These yielded a harvest of prickly fruit with fat nuts every October. A low hedge with a white gate divided the driveway from the garden. The ground rose up, gently, towards the house.

From the end of the drive –about a quarter of a mile away– the house seems to shimmer through a haze of branches, or leaves, according to the season. In snow you see it through a veil of white. The house seems to hover –was it then, or is it now? Do you have to cross a time barrier to reach it? Can anyone go?

On a green April afternoon the sound of children playing echoed through the wood. Was that us long ago, or the children of today? From the gatepost a blackbird poured out its ecstasy, wood pigeons rehearsed their duet and a cock pheasant chuntered in the undergrowth frisking up dry leaves. Are those the sounds of then, or now, and does it matter?

There had been a house here for centuries. The one we were born in had a Jacobean face of rose coloured bricks, tinged with yellow ochre. Like a child's drawing –and my father taught me to draw it– the blue-green front door was its nose. The elegant windows made the eyes. Like ears two chimneys came out of the red pantiled roof. On the roof there was a white lantern housing the bell of a clock which had a blue face that looked across the farm on the south side of the house. The clock's immense seventeenth century works were in the loft. On the other end of the house was a small extension with a thin high chimney poised on its sloping roof. Close by was a small wood with a group of lofty Douglas pines whose rosy trunks caught the light of the setting sun. Our father liked a house, "Framed by woods, but not too close."

This was the home farm for the substantial Langley estate. Its tenure came with my father's job as the newly appointed land agent to the Beauchamp family. He also ran the farm.

There's a snapshot of the house from 1926. I am asleep in the tub shaped carriage pram on the lawn. A huge umbrella shades the pram. The garden looks blooming on a hot summer's day. No one is about. The windows are half curtained in such a way that the house seems to be smiling, its watchful eyes on the baby... The occupants of this house may change, but the house remembers them.

Further pictures make it plain that I was born in the main bedroom, its walls papered with large pink cabbage roses. At a week old I am content with a lot of dark hair. Marjorie looks uncertain. In those days a maternity nurse or a nanny might not work to inspire confidence in a young mother. Rather the reverse.

By three months the snaps show a baby in a white lace dress with a distinct preference for her young nanny's arms. Mother once again evinces a lack of sureness when she does the holding. Assiduously disregarding the three appealing young women on the lawn beside him, my father, handsome in tweed plus fours, is teaching the dog, Skipper, to beg!

There are favourite locations for these regular family photo calls. On the front lawn at Langley, beside clipped topiary bushes at Tor Bryan, Essex –Father's parental home– and under the cedars at Acton Burnell Park, Shropshire, with the Bruce grandparents. Everyone, always, in smart clothes.

At two you can see me pushing a dolls pram. Daddy, smiling, in a flat cap, is sitting on a bench patting the dog. About this time there are snaps at Waxham on the North

Norfolk coast. Here among the sand dunes and the marram grass was a wooden bungalow belonging to friends. It was a simple structure smelling of hot pitch pine.

On the wide sandy beach Daddy with his plus fours rolled up is paddling with me, cigarette in hand. A group of ladies relax on cushions with large hats and dark glasses and more cigarettes. Mother looks distinctly queasy in an unbecoming floppy hat. Sister Mary is on the way.

Naturally, Mary's arrival on May 28th, 1929, changed everything. Marjorie was ill after the birth and confined to bed for a month among the cabbage roses. She had little chance to bond with her new baby. William, probably overwhelmed by a huge sense of responsibility for his growing family, worked even harder. His practice as a land agent was expanding. He visited estates all over England.

The names ran like a litany through my childhood–Foxcote in Gloucestershire, Castle Corby in Cumbria, Ampton and Bramfield in Suffolk.

"Why have they all left me here, standing on the nursery window ledge, held by Nanny? They are all getting into the car with Mary in a long white dress. Mummy said it was a shame I couldn't go because of my cold. I feel so left out".

That same afternoon:

"They've all come back and let me out. This best dress is very thin and the bench hurts my bottom. I'm not comfortable. I like the pattern on Daddy's socks. He's

holding that baby. They've brushed her hair into a cockscomb. It looks silly but she's quiet for once. Now they are going to take photographs. I wish they'd get on with it. I'm very uncomfortable. I can't sit here much longer. They say 'Don't fidget". I'm desperate I WANT TO WEE..."

A year on I was horrified by some of the things they did to Mary, but secretly relieved that it was not me. It was decided that Mary's thumb sucking would do her jaw permanent damage and must be stopped. Frantic to suck she bit her way through the kid gloves they put on her. They tied her wrists to the bars of her cot. Her screaming was awful. In those days Truby King and the magazine 'Nursery World' gave nannies and mothers guidance on child rearing. Much that happened to Mary and me was cruel and abusive. Bowlby and Winnicott were far in the future. Our one secret weapon was to escape.

Once Mary could toddle I was put in charge if we were in the garden. We were given wooden hobby horses. One day we rode them right down the drive. Suddenly it thundered and began to rain – hard. The rain became hailstones and we were pounded by hard little pebbles. It felt vindictive. We were both very frightened. I lifted up the hem of my tweed coat and hid Mary's face against me. We huddled together beside the bluebell wood. Suddenly a car drew up. Albert, the gardener had come to rescue us.

Nanny scolded: "You are a very naughty girl, Ann. Look at your new coats and shoes, soaked. Fancy taking Mary so far when you could see the black clouds".

Nanny made us lie on our beds, for an hour, without books.

When we were older we had ponies and we really escaped... The Langley estate became our world. It was flanked on the east by marshes and the River Yare; on the south by the River Chet. All around were parks and woods. The woods were very important to us.

One day I walked alone up the track we called the Potato Field, and turned into the park. Some way ahead of me, beside the wood, was a very large holly tree. At Christmas time they used to cut boughs off to decorate the house. As I looked at the tree I heard intensely beautiful singing and a flock of birds flew in and out of the branches, but the singing was not birdsong. I realised I was hearing angels singing. The birds rose and fell out of the leaves and circled the tree. I stood gazing and after a while the music ebbed away and the great tree was still.

Journey into Solitude

Marjorie's Diary for 1930

The 1930s

Her diary for 1930 was a large handsome hardback book with *Au Bon Marche, Paris,* in art deco lettering on a cover of cream, grey, black and orange.

No one in the family knows how she came by it. It has interesting notes in French. The overall message is *"tout est moins cher, au Bon Marche"*

It was going to be a very special year. After four years of child bearing and illness, she was going abroad for the very first time. Perhaps she wanted to record it all in an exciting, exotic diary. Perhaps her friend Sib gave it to her.

Her cryptic entries give a picture of her life.

On January 1st:

"Rather tired after the Boileaus' dance. Dined at Christopher's. Farewell to Bobs: off to Australia."

Which translates as: going to a ball given by the Norfolk Hunting set in West Norfolk; dining with a local bachelor; saying good bye to local, rich friends. Going out to dinner, playing bridge and golf, taking the children out to tea, make up a lot of diary entries.

On January 4th she writes:

"Very worn out after all these dissipations. Send Albert to fetch the children from Tor Bryan. Ann and Mary arrive. Ann's cold is throaty. Mary very loud-voiced but spineless as ever."

I was shocked by this entry when I read it. Evidently our mother had avoided a New Year visit to her parents-in-law. She found them intimidating and the house perishingly cold in winter. But she had sent Nanny and her children there. Describing your seven-month-old baby as 'spineless' seems unfeeling. When the nanny falls ill later in the month Marjorie finds the children hard to manage.

"Hectic times in nursery. Aided by Sheila washing up and tubbing Ann".

Sheila is her husband's employer! The next day she records:

"Sheila leaves and kindly sends Ruth, the second housemaid at the Hall, to give me a hand."

My mother showed a real ability to get other people to help her.

Nanny stayed in bed until February 4th. Ruth then leaves, having given everyone her cold. Health is a great preoccupation in Mother's diaries.

Later she writes that they have decided to go for their trip on April 4th.

"I am worried about my leg which still swells. It looks blotchy and odd."

After Mary was born she had phlebitis –a blood clot– and potentially very dangerous.

"Doctor came and said my leg is getting on well. I mustn't be too violent.

I was stupid taking Ann out on the donkey. I shan't walk at all now except for doing the chickens."

I was very frightened riding Rebecca the donkey. I had no saddle or stirrups. Marjorie would bang the road behind us with a walking stick to get Rebecca to trot. It was such misery. Nowadays I see her with an ability to be ruthless at times.

There are a number of diary entries about the chickens. She is often setting a hen on eggs. Years later in therapy, lying on the couch, I "saw" a little chick with its eyes closed. I felt, then, that only a thin membrane separated me from my mother. The boundary between us was thin. I was subsumed into her. Despite the presence of a nanny I did not really separate from my mother.

"I am making Ann a cotton frock and reading up all about Morocco. I think and dream of nothing else. How lovely it will be...... a lovely, lovely spring day. My little Ann is four today. She has a relaxed throat. I take her out in pushchair."

21

I spend the next day in bed. Nanny misses her train back and gets a terrific strafing from William because she was very rude to him. The very next day this somewhat unreliable nanny is dispatched with the children. Albert drove them up to Acton Burnell for a month's stay.

"Sad to see them go. I wish Ann was feeling herself... tomorrow is day of days and off we go. We get ten chicks hatched and set another hen. How many shall I find on my return?"

Of her chicks at Acton Burnell the diary records not another word, until her return three weeks later. Nowhere does she record missing them, sending a postcard or in any way communicating with her parents about them.

She writes about being seasick during a stormy crossing of the Bay of Biscay, Calm seas and sunshine restore her spirits as they cruise past Gibraltar and arrive in Tangiers. Later on she says:

"We are taken round Casablanca to the Arab quarters. New Town is beautiful. The English and Americans have lovely gardens. What wonders the French are doing with their building and gardens and planting everywhere."

They have a 150 mile drive to Marrakesh. The next day:

"Awake to bright sun and deep blue sky over palm trees – a cold wind from the Atlas Mountains which are snow-covered."

22

They reach Asmi in the foothills and start "an amusing" ride on mules but pouring rain sends them back to their hotel. The next day speeding towards Mayagan they are halted as the Grand Prix Auto Race is on their road. Later she feels Rabat is not as interesting as Marrakesh.

Marjorie and William are having a holiday with a Doctor and Mrs Robinson. Several times she mentions that he annoys her. A conversation went something like this:

"William and I left this booking to you. Our room is horrible – dirty and noisy."

Dr Robinson replies:

"I've spoken to the manager and there is nothing he can do about our rooms. He says if we don't like it we can leave. I do not think that's a good idea. Ramadan starts in two days and they don't like us being here. If we leave now we are going to antagonise the manager."

She responds:

"Well, you've certainly left it too late to find us another hotel. It's a pity you booked us in here in the first place... William and I are going for a stroll; we can't possibly sit around in this place. And it's too early to go to bed."

"I really don't think that's a good idea, Marjorie."

Evidently she refused to listen. Maybe William felt a short time away from the Robinsons would be a good idea.

They had not gone far when Abdul, their guide, appeared out of nowhere.

"It is not a good time to make a walk, Mr Petre, Sir… Your lady wife may be in danger.

Out of the corner of her eye Marjorie saw a group of Arab youths picking up stones. Their furtive glances looked menacing. Suddenly a rock hit the ground beside the guide.

"Quick! Quick! back to the hotel."

Abdul grabbed Marjorie's arm and began to hurry her along. William took her other arm.

"Duck! Margie…"

Another stone hit the road beside William.

"Faster! Make haste…" shrieked Abdul.

Panting, they ran across the square towards the hotel. As they fell through the doorway a hail of stones rattled on the front step. They stood up, straightened their clothes and Abdul had disappeared. Marjorie's heart was beating fast. She was sweaty and breathless.

"Why are they so hostile? What have we done to deserve stoning?"

"Ramadan, sweetie, is a very special time for them, rather like Lent for us. They don't want Christians around…"

They go to bed. Her diary goes on:

"In the stinking rat hole of a bedroom I slept very badly. I

*felt hot and feverish and dreamt that Geoffrey Robinson
was throwing plates at a spaniel..."*

In fact, she was developing Fey fever. Sadly, she felt very
ill for most of the rest of their trip. Once on board she crept
into her bunk and was very seasick crossing the Bay.

After a night in London she felt better. William went
back to Norfolk and she travelled up to Acton Burnell. Her
mother, Ismay Bruce, met the train with Ann.

*"April 25th Ann seems so sweet and good. She doesn't
look as well as she should. I shall take her to the E.N.T.
specialist. I hope it's her adenoids so we can get her
right."*

The eventual removal of my tonsils and adenoids did
nothing to cure the pain of that separation from my mummy
and Langley. My acute sense of responsibility for Mary also
seems to have intensified during the period of my parents'
Moroccan adventure.

My parents did not lead exciting lives. It is a mystery
how they got involved in anything as exotic as a trip to
Morocco in 1931. All the artefacts they brought back from
their trip are still around in the family, witnesses perhaps to
the significance of that time for them. I have a set of scenes
painted by a street artist illustrating a world he knew in
bright, primitive colours. These include a snake charmer,
a performing monkey and inside a leather shop.

Marjorie at two

1904

There was a storm in the West Country during the autumn of 1904. My grandmother, Ismay Bruce, lay in bed listening to the wind. Downstairs a shutter was banging. The trees outside the window were shaking their boughs as if demented. Thunder rolled across the moors. An occasional flash of lightning lit up the black tors. Water sloshed along the gutters.

Where's Archie? That shutter must be secured. It'll break the window soon.

Ismay lay in bed cold and miserable. She and Archie had had an awful row that evening. First about money, and then about her fear of another pregnancy. Marjorie, their youngest was two and there were four older children. Ismay, only thirty-two, couldn't bear the thought of another child. Archie was getting more and more insistent that he be allowed back into her bed. She knew that by locking him out she was risking his seeking solace elsewhere. It had happened before, but what could she do?

About midnight the storm grew fiercer. Ismay woke hearing Marjorie cry out from her room along the passage. She put on a wrap and picked up the small paraffin lamp. Out in the corridor, above the noise of the storm, she heard Marjorie calling "Nursie! Nursie!" Why wasn't the girl going to her?

Marjorie was standing up in her cot, shaking the bars and crying desperately. Ismay tried to soothe her. The child was soaking and needed a fresh napkin. That was the nurse's job. She banged on nanny's door.

"Nanny, where are you? Marjorie needs attention. Wake up!"

A clap of thunder right above the house woke all the children in adjoining rooms.

"Nanny the children need you. Wake up!"

She opened the nurse's door. In the background Marjorie wailed hysterically and all the children were calling. Ismay was transfixed as nanny slithered naked from her bed. Ismay pulled back the covers and there was Archie, also naked. Even in her rage and shock she was touched by his pathetic inadequacy, in a foetal position trying to cover his small, flaccid penis.

None knew better than Ismay the urgency of Archie's sexual needs. She was moved by his vulnerability. She enjoyed their love-making but it exacted such terrible penalties –five births and three miscarriages to date.

"Archie! There's a shutter needs fixing downstairs… Nanny, see to the children, then pack your bags and leave first thing, before breakfast."

So, in an instant, like the lightning, my toddler mother suffered a devastating loss. I grew up knowing of her misery. She had woken next day to find her beloved Nursie gone without a word. No one explained her absence. She was taken care of by a maid. Although only two it seems she was quite aware of the whispering among her siblings. She sensed something awful had happened. Presumably the whole story came out when she was much older. Ismay made efforts, but in contemporary parlance, never bonded with her. She gave her a large toy monkey which Marjorie hated. She ached with longing for her lovely Nursie. Nothing and no one, it seems, ever really made up for the loss of that first care-giver.

No doubt Archibald missed Nursie too. He may have found her beautiful and kind. She was probably good with the children. Ismay had so much that preoccupied her. Maybe Grandpa appreciated Nursie for the things Ismay didn't or couldn't do.

It was part of the family story that Grandpa seduced young women employees, and Granny always forgave him. I have no record of his early life, except that his father was a Welsh clergyman related to Lord Aberdare, a peer from Glamorganshire. His mother was French, an Olivier, related to the famous Lawrence. It seems that Archibald Dacre Austin was given no professional training. He came to excel at those country pursuits – hunting, shooting and fishing – that require money rather than make it.

Grandpa had some kind of ability to be in touch with past events and earlier inhabitants of a house. In one of their Devonshire homes the children had been frightened by strange bangings at night. My mother told me that one night my grandfather lay in wait and was confronted by a small misshapen man in a monk's habit. Grandpa asked him to go away and stop being a nuisance, whereupon the presence hit my grandfather with a knotted rope as he ran past him. After that encounter the noises ceased.

When grandpa was at Acton Burnell he often saw, in the evening, an old couple dressed in clothes of an earlier period, walking beside the long herbaceous border.

Journey into Solitude

Daddy

1930s

"Daddy is dying on a table by the bluebell wood. As I walk up to the house I am overwhelmed with racking, tearless sobs......

Then I am beside him again. I gaze at his body which is that of a baby. His skin looks charred, blackish, withered as if burnt.

I look at his penis and marvel that I came from there. He stirs. I say: 'I'll stay here right to the end.'

He wakes and as an adult half sits up looking at me with great sweetness. He says that he is cold. I go to fetch a blanket."

Dream Journal, July 27th, 1999

"Ann, Ann, Come here!"

Aged five or six I was in the nursery bathroom, crouched behind some curtains. Daddy sounded very cross and I was very scared. The room had only lately been made into a second bathroom. It had been the night nursery. Curtains covered a space in the corner. Clothes were hung behind them.

Nanny had made these new curtains. They smelt fresh and had a pattern of blue, green and brown squares that I disliked. The room smelt of soap and water. I felt very sick.

"Ann. Where are you? Come out!"

I knew why he was so angry. I had been waiting for this all day. That morning I had been reading a Janet and John book with Mummy. Usually reading wasn't difficult but the new words at the start of this chapter were: "where". "whether". "which". I found 'wh' impossibly difficult. Not being able to read the words had provoked a very rare confrontation with Mummy.

She got very upset and said – again, this was a rare occurrence – "I shall tell Daddy when he gets home."

For some time I had known what the deal was with Daddy. Probably the contract was there, vaguely, from the beginning. It had got clearer since Mary's arrival and Mummy's poor health. The Agreement, never verbalised, of course, went like this: 'You will continue to be Daddy's very special Ann if, and only if, you are good and help look after Mummy.'

On that particular evening the danger of conditional love was made very plain to me.

I moved further in behind the curtains. He pulled me out.

"You played your mother up at your lessons this morning."

A statement not a question. He bent me over his knee –he was wearing his usual rough tweed plus fours. He took off his hard-soled red indoor shoe and hit me hard, twice, on my bottom.

I looked up at his furious face. His eyes were bulging, his mouth open, and his tongue glistening. Inside his mouth it was pink and moist. I didn't know the word but it felt sexual. It felt grossly indecent, unfair, humiliating, but, above all, world shattering. I hated my mother for telling tales. I hated him for not asking me for my side of things. I hated and suddenly despised him for making me his companion in caring for my mother and then treating me like a child.

What was I meant to be? An adult or a child? I certainly grew up schooled to be 'unselfish'; to put my mother and sisters first.

It got worse. By next morning all the farm seemed to have heard about what had happened in the bathroom. I never discovered who leaked the news. I suspected Nanny. The horseman, normally a kindly man, teased me.

"So, Miss Ann, we hear the Captain gave you a good thrashing. You must have been a naughty girl." The unpleasant cowman with the yellow face leered. The humiliation and rage I felt were worse because I couldn't do anything about the situation. The farm hands knew my father to be a stern and irascible man. Maybe they were relieved to hear of someone else being his victim this time.

When I reflect on the bathroom incident nowadays I am aware that I knew, at the time, that he wasn't just angry with me. I was standing in for other people as well. He never hit me again, nor, as far as I know, did he hit my sisters, Mary or Helen. After this incident I became very scared of him.

It was probably at about this time that I started to live a secret life in the wood at the back of the house. A ridge about a metre high curved through the wood. Perhaps it was a relic of some early drainage system. Along the crest of this ridge ran an untrodden path. Tall ash and sycamore trees grew from the sides of the ridge, their roots exposed by weathering. At one place the roots of three trees grew so close that they made an enclosed bower. This became my refuge. As the trees swayed and whispered in the wind I knew God was there in the treetops. I told Him my miseries. I asked Him not to let me become like the grown ups but to keep me as I was.

When I was seven I was allowed to bicycle to weekday mass in Bungay, seven and a half miles away. It was not just piety that motivated these expeditions; it was also the sense of adventure and freedom. I didn't have an alarm clock so I had to rely on banging my head on the pillow six times before I went to sleep. My bedroom window rattled in the wind and woke me. Sometimes it was still dark as I pedalled through Chedgrave and on past Loddon church. The lane then wound through fields until I reached Ditchingham Dam and the River Waveney. Up the steep hill to the church. With the mass over I came home slowly. I stopped on Ditchingham heath to eat my sandwiches as the sun warmed my back and skylarks spiralled up from the gorse bushes.

I wonder whether Daddy knew of these expeditions. Did he approve of my solitary church going?

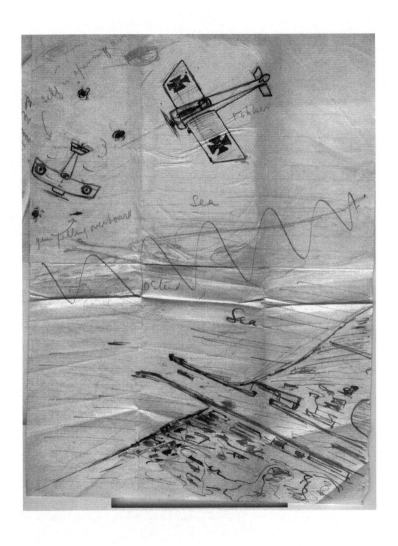

Tor Bryan, Ingatestone

1880 – 1941

In the 1880s my father's father, Sebastian Henry Petre, built a fine house on the edge of Ingatestone village in Essex. He extended the existing Heybridge House into a larger, grander house and re-named it Tor Bryan, after the Devonshire village, the birthplace of Sir William Petre. This ancestor was considered to be 'a founder of the family's rank and fortunes'. His father, John, had been a tanner but William rose to become secretary of state to four successive Tudor monarchs. Sebastian's cousin, Lord Petre, lived a mile away in Ingatestone Hall, across the railway tracks of the new L.N.E.R.

My grandfather, a solicitor in the family firm, had many interests, including architecture. He was a keen supporter of the Arts and Crafts movement so Tor Bryan became a fine example of a William Morris house.

The house was built of small, deep red, tudor-style bricks. The gable ends were made of gleaming white wood. In the British Architect Magazine in 1891, T. Raffles Davison described the dining-room:

'Here all is permanent, solid, architectural decoration,

high oak panelling, plaster frieze and admirably-modelled plaster ceiling, red-brick mullioned windows, polished oak floor and mahogany furniture.'

Many other rooms had original William Morris wallpapers. The article writer was delighted to meet Mr S H Petre describing him as a gentleman who:

'...appreciated professional work, both old and new' and who had more thorough and sound architectural ideas than: 'the bulk of architects themselves.'

Sebastian had a well equipped workshop built for his children. Here they all learnt and practised a variety of crafts including etching, cabinet making and smelting.

My father born in 1888 was in the exact middle of seven children. There was a palindrome of siblings – a daughter, five sons and then a final daughter. I wonder whether William felt a bit isolated among his siblings. The older pair, Henry and Edward were great friends, as were the younger pair, Bernard and Jack.

An early portrait photograph shows William at about four in Edwardian fancy dress. He has long blonde ringlets and is pushing a wheelbarrow with a trowel and fork. Does this suggest a life's passion with growing things? It seems that at about this age each boy would progress from nursery to schoolroom, no doubt having long hair cut off on the way. The child must have experienced some sense of loss of the familiar. The children were born at two to three-yearly intervals and must have had less to do with Mother once they reached the schoolroom with the governess.

The boys all went to Jesuit boarding schools. William told my mother that he was always in trouble at Mount St Mary's. "I was beaten every day...but it made a man of me." Even as a child I wondered about that. Was it true? What was its meaning? Presumably he was high spirited and rebellious, and like his brothers, prepared to take the consequences of his actions.

At home the lads were into feats of daring, like riding their motor bikes round the coping of a nearby railway bridge. They made their own aeroplane and in 1910 it was exhibited in the aero show at Olympia. They flew thirty yards before crashing it.

In 1912, only four years after Bleriot crossed the channel in a monoplane, Edward, aged twenty-six, training to be an engineer, attempted the first non-stop London to Edinburgh flight in a Martin-Handasyde monoplane. Caught in a gale blowing off the Cleveland Hills in North Yorkshire, he crashed near Marske-by-the-sea and died instantly with a broken neck. The flight and the subsequent inquest remained national news for over a month. His mother collected all the press-cuttings into a bound book.

William and the other brothers were fliers in the Great War. Jack, the youngest, and by all accounts a bit of a lad as well as being handsome and dashing, was killed when the wing of his Sopwith Pup broke off while he was demonstrating flying to a class of cadets in Flanders in 1917. His letters home, also bound by his mother into a book, show his easy relationship with her and the rest of his family.

"Has my car arrived home yet? I hope so. Please see that it is taken care of. Please write soon." ..."Have just come down from chasing Boches with my tribe of scouts."

Later in a P.S.

"Have just been told I am to receive Croix de Guerre on Thursday. Hope to goodness the general does not treat me to any kissing stunts as he did the last people who got it."

What was it like to lose two of your brothers, and later your youngest sister? William and Henry were reserved men who kept their feelings hidden. I never remember my father talking about his siblings' deaths, or his experiences of the war in the RFC. He survived and like many others was silent about what he had witnessed and endured. He probably believed in making the best of things, but he was no extrovert. During the thirties while he was working hard to establish his estate agency business, he was aware, like Churchill – whom he both resembled and admired – that "The storm clouds are gathering".

Perhaps his reluctance to share his deepest feelings was inherited from his mother. His father seems to have been more easy going and extrovert.

Elise Sibeth married Sebastian Petre with a grand London wedding in 1881. In the list of presents which seems de rigueur in the Times Wedding Reports of the day, it says, after all the gifts from the main guests, that the servants of the Sibeth household gave the couple a silver and blue china biscuit case.

My grandmother was an ardent admirer of her husband's family and its ancient faith. She worked hard to imbue her children, and then her grandchildren, with family pride and lofty ideals. She left me in no doubt that to die a martyr was the supreme accolade. I grew up hearing, and believing, that 'Obedience is better than Sacrifice', that 'Life is not a Bed of Roses', and 'It is far better to Give than to Receive.' Elise seems to have been a strong influence on my mother who became, in ways, 'more Petre than a Petre'.

My grandmother's spirituality no doubt deepened with the successive losses of two sons and then, in 1929, of her daughter Sybil, the youngest in the family. Already a talented artist, Sybil died of a kidney disease in Italy, separated from her five year old daughter, my first cousin, Elizabeth. I remember my grandmother –called by us, Daadie– always wearing black clothes and a black hat. On the landings at Tor Bryan there were altars with statues of Our Lady, the Sacred Heart and the Saints. As children we knelt beside our grandmother, on a prie-dieu, reciting prayers appropriate to each shrine.

Grandfather, called Da Da, built a new Catholic church on land next to Tor Bryan. Stained glass windows were dedicated to their three dead children.

Daadie had some of the characteristics of Lady Marchmain in 'Brideshead Revisited.' These included devotion to the Catholic Faith and to Family Honour, deep piety, asceticism and self-denial.

One Easter Sunday when I was about seven I gazed up at the stained glass windows above the altar and read the names of my dead uncles and my aunt. Suddenly I became convinced that God was calling me to dedicate my life to Him. He wanted me to become a Little Sister of the Poor when I grew up. I promised Him that I would.

Daadie called Tor Bryan 'Liberty Hall' and beside the prayers and church going we did, as children, have fun and a fair amount of freedom. Cousin Elizabeth, nicknamed Lela, was two years older and far more adventurous than I was. She was brought up at Tor Bryan. We had a great time building dams in the stream that ran out of the lakes. Lela frightened me when she said that Bonzo, the fierce male swan, could break your leg with a wing beat.

In 1932 a fashionable roadhouse was built opposite Tor Bryan. They added a wonderful swimming pool all aquamarine and cream paint with a clock tower. A perfect example of a thirties lido, where we all learnt to swim.

From about that time I have a memory of being in the library and watching Da Da tip up a Chippendale chair to explain something about its workmanship to my father. I remember my father's attentiveness to being taught something by his father. Astonishing!

Da Da died in 1934. Daadie, Aunt Mary – the unmarried daughter, and Lela stayed on at Tor Bryan until Daadie's death in 1946. Eventually the house and grounds were bought by a property developer. The lake remained but the house was razed to the ground in 1961. Some of the fine trees were incorporated in the 'landscaped' housing estate.

The loss of both Tor Bryan and Acton Burnell to our family seems due to sociological and political changes and the crippling size of death duties. Both houses were too large for one family by the 1940s. Acton Burnell Park survived because it was bought by an institution. It seems sad that the conservation movement came too late to save Tor Bryan. But the Catholic church built by Da Da is still in use today

Nanny

1926 – 1941

There was a nanny at Langley Hall Farm until I was nearly sixteen. Nanny Cooke looked after me from birth until I was four. She seems, from the 1930 diary, to have had much ill health. She was said at this time, by the doctor, to suffer from nervous debility and slight kidney trouble. Mother wrote:

> *"Her health now is her reason for leaving... she worries herself to a skeleton".*

Nanny was probably conscientious about her responsibilities.

How far she bonded with Mary it is hard to know. She looked after her from birth to age one. It is likely that we both missed her as a constant presence in the nursery. The photos show her as a pretty young woman in a white dress and apron, a black belt, a large white collar with a floppy black bow. She holds babies with competence and confidence.

How far did the Moroccan holiday and the stay at Acton Burnell contribute to her leaving? She was in charge of a young baby and a four year old in a very large, unfamiliar house, answerable to grandparents. She had had a serious telling off from my father on the eve of the departure for Acton Burnell. She left Langley soon after our return.

Her successor, Nanny Walker, wore a stylish black cloche hat and was also young and pretty. She took us for walks along the Back Lane to a large patch of grass beside the main road from Loddon to Norwich. The ostensible purpose of the walk was to buy us 'snowfrute' ice creams from the Walls or Eldorado man who pedalled out ten miles from Norwich with a box of assorted ices. Nanny seemed to enjoy talking to these men who must have been glad to rest awhile. The buses were also delayed while Nanny talked to the driver and the conductor. She remains in my memory as a friendly, undemanding Nanny with an exciting aura of flightiness. Sadly she didn't last long. Had someone noticed our walks and reported her to my mother?

I have a clear memory of the afternoon Mary and I were taken by Minnie, the house parlour maid, down to the local shops. Our mission was to buy a welcome present for the new Nanny. I remember examining a large card of hair slides. Albert has gone to the other side of the county to collect her. Even before she arrived I was aiming to 'get on the right side of her' –a tactic I was to use a lot over the next ten years.

"It felt a bit strange leaving Mother and Father and the village. Nice to strike out on my own, with no bossy head nanny or governess. I'll miss Lady C. My new mistress isn't a bit like her Ladyship, judging from my interview.

The timid sort. She's got it all to learn. 'Don't let anyone get the better of you', Mother said. 'Show them from Day One who's in charge in the nursery'...

I shall miss Harry and Nancy. These new children are much younger. Ann is going to start lessons soon with her mother. I'd have liked a baby, but you can't have everything straight off. Who knows, one may come along once they realise they've got a firm and reliable nanny......She said I could knit for them and do fancy sewing, like making smocks...I'll get my list of duties approved at once...Mother said it was important that I do no housework outside the nurseries......no bits of cooking or washing up when the maids are off duty...

There's only a cook and a maid...Albert here doubles up as gardener and chauffeur... not like up at the hall."

She sighed and stretched her short legs, glancing at Albert.

"I don't take to him......stubborn. Shut up like a clam when I asked him about the master."

She was twenty-four, short and stout. She longed to be slim. She yearned for a boyfriend. She was to dominate our household for the next decade. She respected my father, vehemently disliked Albert and bullied everyone else.

The tortoiseshell hair slide didn't do us much good.

Like Mary Poppins her nurseries were spick and span. Clothes tidied themselves at a look. Like Mary she had a bun and an upturned nose, but her complexion was swarthy. Her accent was broad Norfolk overlaid with gentry-speak. She liked to be hugged but her body, encased in a corset, was unyielding. Her smacks made your limb glow.

One day, soon after her arrival, Mary and I were in the night nursery 'having a rest'. This hour immediately before or after lunch was entirely for the benefit of the grown ups. We were meant to lie on our beds without books or toys and keep quiet.

Nanny had the hour off. This particular day, knowing she was downstairs, we were not resting but romping. We were going round the room, climbing on the furniture, our feet not touching the blue lino.

"Pretend it's a rough sea, Mary"

Unfortunately, just as I made a long leap onto Mary's bed, Nanny looked up from the backyard below the window.

"Lie down at once…I'm coming up to give you both a good smack."

The waiting was awful. It lasted a long time. She smacked Mary who howled. She came over to my bed, grasped my right arm and smacked it hard. Fascinated I watched the skin change colour from pink to angry red.

This distracted me from crying.

Worse was to come. She had an unerring knack of discovering other people's secrets. She was intensely inquisitive and always wanted to know what was going on. She seemed to resent the time I spent with my mother.

On one occasion I was saving to go on an expedition with Mummy. In my secret place, in the wood behind the house, I had dug a hole in the bank.

Here among the roots of the sycamores I had hidden a red tin. In the tin were four half crowns, a present from my godfather, Uncle Henry, on his last visit. No one knew of this place, not even Mary. It was my thinking place.

"Where's that money?" She asked one day.

"It's...um...it's in a bank"

"Which bank?"

"The one in the Plantation".

"Don't tell lies. There's no bank there. You cannot keep money outside. Fetch it in, at once."

She'd made it all sound ridiculous. She had spoiled something. She had come much too close to my secret place. Soon she'd leave me with nothing.

I hated her all-seeing eye. I hated myself for not being able to stand up to her. I was aware she manipulated my mother too.

"That girl is two-faced. Running to her mother all the time. These so-called educational visits. Fancy taking her to be in an historical pageant in Ambleside. A waste of time and money having a special dress made so she can be Queen Margaret of Scotland... As if the child didn't have enough silly romantic ideas already.

Mary's different. More spirit. I like that. It gives you more to work on… When she's a bit older I shall ask Madam whether I can give her these P.N.E.U. lessons that Ann is taught…"

P.N.E.U. was the Parents National Education Union with headquarters in Cumbria. It provided an excellent curriculum for home teaching.

In 1936 I was given a Brownie Box camera for my tenth birthday. I photographed the household, outside the front door before my parents left for their second –and last– foreign holiday. They went to the Italian Lakes and it rained the whole time.

As a big treat Mary and I were taken to stay with Nanny's parents.

Nanny's father was a farm labourer on the West Norfolk estate and they lived in a two up, two down tied cottage.

The stairs were as steep as a ladder. Any bathing was done in a zinc bath put in front of the kitchen range. The privy was down a path through the vegetable garden. It smelt and everything dropped into a dark pit far below. The paper was squares of newspaper stuck on a nail, rough on your bottom.

I slept alone in the small back bedroom that had been Nanny's. There were few books on the mantelpiece. I struggled to read "Tom Brown's Schooldays." The bed had a rough white bedspread with tassels. On the washstand were a china water jug and basin and soap dish. The pattern of flowers on these also decorated the potty under the bed. Out of the window I could see water meadows and a distant river.

Mary slept next door with Nanny in the parents' bedroom. Where did they sleep? Perhaps on the kitchen couch? The black range had a small fire and several ovens. Mrs French served wonderful roast lunches of beef, gravy, Yorkshire pudding, potatoes and vegetables from their garden. "He'll get his after" she'd say, indicating her small, silent husband. He had two fingers missing from each hand, caught in farm machinery. He had his meal backwards. First a whole plateful of Yorkshire and gravy, then the potatoes and vegetables and finally the meat.

Nanny's mother was a tall, stately woman with dark skin and flashing black eyes. Her thick dark hair was piled high and held in place by combs. She always wore a long black dress with a crocheted black shawl. There was something Latin about her. Tradition has it that some Spanish sailors wrecked on this coast after the Armada, may have added their genes to the indigenous population. Nanny seemed to shrink in her own home. She was much quieter and less bossy. She was the youngest with four siblings. At home Mrs French was queen.

When Lady C heard of our visit she very kindly asked us up to the hall for tea. It was a magnificent Tudor mansion. We went but felt uncomfortable as if we were changing sides. I was glad to get back to the cottage. For the moment it was familiar and home.

Eventually Nanny tried to teach Mary to read, write and do sums. Mary was not keen to learn and found everything difficult. Punishing Mary was singularly unsuccessful. When she got to boarding school in 1939 she had a very hard time. Only as an adult did she realise she was severely dyslexic.

Nanny writes to her mother:

"August 31st. Wonderful news! After all these years, Mrs P told me today she's expecting a baby next spring. She's asked me to stay on to look after him. Mary will go to school in September. Madam thinks it will be a son. Ann apparently wants to call him Charles or James Stuart. I wouldn't have told the children yet…"

Next spring she writes:

"April 25th, 1939. Helen Elizabeth born this morning. A beautiful 8 pound baby with a mass of red gold hair and green eyes. I'm as happy as I've ever been. A baby, at last, in my nursery."

Marjorie's diary for 1941 records a very snowy winter. The house is cold. Helen, nearly two, has frequent chest infections. Nanny writes home:

"Up all night with Helen. She coughs and coughs and can't get her breath, poor little thing. Madam found me asleep at 7 am in the chair by her cot. She says she doesn't know how I do it, night after broken night. I think Madam wishes she could do more but Helen seems to need me there all the time when she's this poorly."

In her diary Marjorie constantly records Nanny's devotion to Helen, especially when Helen gets seriously ill with bronchitis. She writes:

"January 30ᵗʰ, Helen very coughy and miserable and cries a lot. Nanny nurses her by the fire and they get to bed at last at 1 am...

Poor Nanny, so tired and got a bad chest herself...Italians fleeing before us in North Africa now, wholesale. Very few raids here lately.

Nanny looks deadbeat. I wish I was in Nanny's place beside my lamb".

For the rest of that year, after Helen recovers, the diary hints at the tug of war going on between Nanny and Marjorie for possession of Helen. For brief periods, when Nanny goes home, Helen seems to settle with her mother – but as soon as Nanny is back Marjorie feels she loses her again. It was not until December that Marjorie summoned the necessary courage to give Nanny notice.

Nanny wrote:

"I cannot believe it after all I've done for this family. Today she gave me notice. Says she can manage on her own now. I'm to leave after Christmas. I feel very ill. The Master was kind, he came and spoke to me after he got home from work. I think he would rather I stayed. He wonders whether Madam can cope without me. I find it hard to stop crying. Helen keeps asking:

'What matter, Nanny?" What can I say? 'My heart is broken, my Pet..."

Nanny's departure was delayed by the onset of atrocious weather. She wept continuously. She finally left in January 1942, ending the reign of Nannies at Langley.

Boarding School

1937 – 1943

My best friend Polly said:

"I have to go down the West Wing to have a bath. Will you come with me?"

It was the start of my second year at a convent boarding school. My father managed the nuns' small estate.

We walked quietly along the seniors' corridor. The old floor creaked.

"Why aren't the lights on?"

We reached the swing doors. The two bathrooms and six lavatories lay beyond, in complete darkness.

Suddenly, I was grabbed by rough, unseen hands and blindfolded. I was held by my arms and legs and dragged towards the bathrooms.

I screamed and a hand was clamped over my mouth. Many hands hoisted me up and then I was lowered into a bath. I heard whispers. A door closed softly. Complete silence. I was very cold and my heart thumped.

There was a muffled noise from the next door bathroom.

I waited a few more minutes then dragged off the blindfold. A faint light was coming from the window. There was a piece of paper in my hand. I clambered out of the bath.

I felt my way to the door, and opened it. I was surprised to see Polly standing there. She clutched my arm.

"Have they gone?"

We waited listening. Far away the supper bell clanged. Polly ran ahead. We were just in time for the supper line up. As we moved into the refectory I realised I was still clutching the piece of paper. I stuffed it into my blazer pocket.

Supper was my favourite –thick lentil soup with fried croutons, followed by apple pie and custard. I was ravenous. I noticed Polly ate little.

Later in bed I remembered the paper. By the dim dormitory light, badly written in uneven capitals, I read:

"This is your first warning. We are sick of you being a goody and getting such high marks in class. CHANGE or the GANG of SPIDERS will strike again…"

The lights went out and for the first time I wished I was back at Langley Hall Farm. I cried myself to sleep.

After that, for no very clear reason Polly and I stopped being friends. I felt uneasy about her and the West Wing bathrooms. Had she acted as a decoy? There were other changes. I invented a game.

We were supplied with sheets of blotting paper in assorted colours. I tore off a corner and chewed it into a mushy lump. I placed this on the end of my ruler and flicked it upwards as the teacher turned away to write on the blackboard. With luck the lump stuck on the ceiling to be joined by others in assorted colours. It was fun. Others joined in. Soon we had made a mosaic.

One day, out of the blue, I was called to the head's office. She was very small, icy, terrifyingly courteous and curiously low voiced. This morning she was seething as well. She advanced from behind her desk. I retreated back to the wall next to her crucifix. Still she came on, until her face was a few inches from mine. Her stiff wimple scratched my cheek. Her breath and black clothes smelt stale. Her voice was barely controlled.

"Ann, are you responsible for the total devastation of your newly decorated classroom?"

What did she mean?

"The ceiling is covered in marks!"

In a flash a good game had become a criminal act.

"Yes. I did invent a…"

Who had sneaked?

"We are very disappointed in you. So far you have done so well. What is your father going to say?"

Oh! God, don't bring him into this. I got a double bathroom flashback.

"How many others were there? Five. Tell me their names… At break you will count all the marks. Divide the total by six. Have that number of discipline marks each."

We counted the hateful spots. There were thirty-seven. I got the extra discipline mark. Unfortunately, it so happened that five of us belonged to St Thomas More's house. At the end of that term the Mores lost the silver house shield to Blessed Margaret Pole, on account of our discipline marks.

I was deeply in love with the More's house captain –a beautiful full-breasted sixteen year old with a mop of lustrous black curls. She gazed at me sadly:

"Oh! Petre what <u>have</u> you done?"

A good outcome of this disgrace was that I was never bothered by the Spiders again. I also learnt something of the joy of being bad, not good all the time.

In 1939 Helen Elizabeth was born and war broke out. Mary joined me at school. She was miserable. She missed the ponies at home. She couldn't do the lessons and she was persecuted by her elderly form teacher.

I was given permission to tuck her in. She was a junior and her bedtime coincided with our supper. She wept every night, that first term, and clung to me so I always slipped into supper late. After a few weeks the presiding nun spotted me. She questioned me and said that Mary was quite settled now, and I was not to go and see her in the dormitory any more.

I felt furious and miserable. The lentil soup with croutons, apple pie and custard did nothing for me that evening. I had let Mary down. She was very unhappy and needed me. It was no good writing to Mummy; they were all too busy at Langley with Helen and the war.

June 1940

The school, the community and various hangers-on left the comparative safety of the Eastern Counties and evacuated to a crumbling mansion owned by an impecunious Catholic peer in a rural part of the Midlands.

On our first night there, before we had begun to unpack, Coventry, fifteen miles away, was bombed. The nuns hadn't had time to look at the cellars so we were told to crouch under what would be the dining room tables. The windows had no curtains. The eastern sky provided a fantastic firework display. I have no memory of being frightened. With every 'crump' the overhead cutlery rattled.

I was fourteen and I didn't like a being a senior and expected to set a good example. Half the school had left. Parents had sent their children to safety in America. It was all rather dull. Adults seemed worried and preoccupied. Reading my mother's diary, later, I realised that many, beside my parents, feared that if there was an invasion they might never see their children again. Our mother used precious petrol coupons to drive over from Norfolk to see us several times during 1940 and 1941.

On the nuns' side of this decayed mansion there was a vast faux baronial hall. On summer evenings the whole community – choir nuns, lay sisters, gardeners etc., would assemble round a small radio set to listen to the news. Up on the first floor us, older girls, were allowed to creep along the corridor. We crouched behind the banisters and listened to the voice below. We thrilled to Churchill's speeches...

"We shall fight them on the beaches…" he boomed.

Beaches? I thought about making sand castles at Waxham, swimming to the raft at Aldeburgh…

Many sense memories of that long hot summer remain. The dusty ballroom curtains that couldn't be touched or they might fall apart; fungus and mould among the cherubs on the ornate plaster ceilings; the acute shortage of lavatories and the dwindling water supply. I still occasionally dream of a blocked lavatory behind a fine carved door. This is the backcloth for my pubescent yearning for Bridie and the sense of being excluded from something very important.

My new best friend was Bridie. She was a few months older than me. She was stunning in a full Irish way. Tall, slim, large brown eyes, moist like a heifer's, and well-developed breasts. She'd started her periods at eleven. For the rest of school life I loved Bridie and she loved an older girl called Marie – also Irish.

Bridie suffered from severe nose bleeds and hay fever. That June the sun shone and the country air was filled with grass seed and the scent of elder and overblown roses. We didn't have dormitories. We slept on mattresses on the polished floors of state rooms. One evening I had permission to go to my locker to fetch a sanitary towel. As I pushed open the heavy door to the ballroom I saw Bridie on her mattress. She was not alone. She was sobbing hysterically, her arms tight round Marie. Marie lying beside Bridie was stroking her hair in an attempt to soothe her and talking in a low voice. The tableau was disturbing.

"No, No, I'll never let you go..." Bridie gulped and sobbed. They were too engrossed to see me. I crept out, profoundly shocked. Later Bridie told me that Marie was going to join the community in the autumn. I hoped things might change with Marie in the novitiate, but they didn't really.

That autumn a beautiful new teacher came to the school. She was tall and very thin with an air of mystery about her. Rumour had it that she had wanted to be a nun but she was too delicate.

She was an Oxford graduate. Very soon she decided that I should set my sights on getting into Oxford.

"So the nuns think you can get into Oxford?" He looks very pleased.

"Yes, Daddy, but I need to have more coaching in Latin and essay writing."

"Do they think you'll get a scholarship?"

"I don't think so." He looks worried.

"Oh! Well! I suppose I could manage the fees out of income. How much will they come to in a year?"

"I'm afraid I don't know Daddy, but I'll find out...Will it be alright for me to leave boarding school this summer and come home and go to Norwich High School for Girls to help me get through the entrance exam?"

Presumably he said "Yes.

Acton Burnell

1920 – 1939

"I am looking after two little girls and a baby...we have to make the journey back. This involves being on the roof at Acton Burnell and going through a door into one of the great glass skylights. It's hard to get through the door because a strong wind is blowing boughs of a huge thorn tree across it The boughs are like a prickly octopus threatening to lacerate the children.

It's a very dark night...I must get him to cut the thorns back...

The little girls turn into babies and soil themselves. I cannot manage on my own..."

(A dream during therapy)

My mother's mother, Ismay Ursula Annunciata – (born on the feast of the Annunciation, March 25th 1872) – inherited Acton Burnell Park on the death of her father, Sir Walter Smythe, the 8th baronet, in 1919. Thus ended the peripatetic wanderings of Ismay and Archibald Bruce. Since marriage in 1894 they had lived in many places, from West Virginia to Ireland, the West Country and Aldeburgh, Suffolk, during the war. It must have been a great relief to settle at last into a fine Palladian mansion with a modest estate in Shropshire. The baronetcy, founded in 1660, virtually ended then, as Ismay's older brother, Edward, the 9th baronet, was in the care of the Master of Lunacy. The story went that he had been hit on the head during a cricket match as a young man. This seems to have robbed him of his reason and his speech.

The estate was saddled with heavy death duties. Ismay inherited a large Edwardian-type of establishment. Probably stringent economies were required. They were never put into place.

The house had four floors. 'Uncle Eddie' was housed on the third floor, in his own set of rooms, and was cared for by the butler. There was a feeling of 'Jane Eyre' about this arrangement. Ismay's mother, the dowager Lady Smythe had her set of rooms, overlooking the gardens, at the other end of the house. Attached to the house was a large Catholic chapel, smaller, but rather like the one described in Waugh's 'Brideshead Revisited.' The Smythes were an old Catholic family and many on the estate came to Sunday Mass.

Indoor staff included three liveried men servants, an Irish cook, a Scottish housekeeper and various house parlour maids, kitchen and scullery maids. The bill for their keep was inflated by food being sent out, discreetly, to the villagers by their relations in the servants' hall!

The Smythes of Acton Burnell were clients of Blount, Lynch and Petre – my grandfather's firm – years before my father became agent to the estate. In those days Catholic landed families, as well as monastic houses, used the services of Catholic legal practices. If clients and their professional advisers intermarried, conflicts of interest must have sometimes arisen.

In the years before she inherited Acton Burnell, Ismay Bruce used to write to her father for money. A letter from Sebastian Petre, as the family's solicitor, dated 17th August 1915, was in one of the small drawers of the desk I inherited from my mother.

In beautiful copperplate Sebastian says he has discussed Ismay's financial situation with her father. Sir Walter has reluctantly agreed to pay her a quarterly allowance to replace the intermittent sums of money he has been giving her.

It is likely that Ismay and Archie thought the estate was more of a golden goose than it was. Money denied them was put down to Sir Walter's parsimony or Sebastian's undue caution. In fact there was not a large amount of disposable income available.

Certainly expense was not spared when it came to Marjorie's wedding in 1925. She was their youngest child and the only one married from Acton Burnell.

The Shrewsbury Chronicle described the event:

Wedding at Acton Burnell

Guard of Honour armed with Hayforks

...The bride looked charming in her dress of white satin Beaute, with a crystal girdle, and a train of old Brussels Lace, lent by the bridegroom's mother, Mrs Petre. From her Russian headdress of orange blossom fell an old Brussels lace veil given by her mother.

There were six adult bridesmaids with Russian head-dresses, and "the tiny page looked very pretty in his Georgian suit..."

The 120 guests had been generous with their presents. One gave a hunter, another a side-saddle. There were silver entrée dishes from the staff of Acton Burnell Estate, a coalport dinner service from the Acton Burnell Tenants, a silver coffee pot from the staff of the Langley Estate, and a silver fruit dish from the Langley Tenants. These last lovely things are still in use in the family today.

Henry Petre, William's older brother, went into the family firm. My mother made me aware as a child that Henry and my father worked hard to manage the economy of the Acton Burnell estate. No doubt at times there was tension between them and my grandparents. In different parts of the country my father worked unremittingly to preserve estates and not squander their assets. He was passionate about his love for the land and the need for careful husbandry.

For us as children visiting Acton Burnell was the crowning joy of the year. Every August our family left Norfolk to stay, for up to six weeks, in Shropshire. First there was a long day's journey, with Albert driving the car packed with people and luggage. Lunch was always at the Bridge Hotel in Huntingdon. The next stop was for tea in Craven Arms. By now we were getting very excited looking out for the Wrekin. Then there would be distant glimpses of the Lawley and the Caradoc near Church Stretton – sleek dark green shapes like whales, totally foreign and exotic to our Norfolk eyes.

In the early evening we drove down a small winding lane towards the village of black and white cottages, and, yes, there it was – the Hall, honey coloured with a three columned portico and countless windows, set against the purple backdrop of Acton Burnell Hill.

By the front door stood Granny and Grandpa and Cousin Nancy – my grandfather's 'secretary' – a dachshund and a spaniel. The butler, footman and hallboy took the luggage and we all moved into the marble entrance hall. It smelt different to home – spacious, cool and grand.

Soon Mary and I would escape to go up to the castle. This was a ruined fortified manor house built in the 1280s. It was being slowly restored by the Ministry of Works. There were mounds of bricks. Here we had a dock leaf factory where we pounded the leaves and caught the juice in walnut shells. The juice was the perfect cure for nettle stings. Every summer we hurried to find the shells left in a secret place last year. Nanny never discovered this game. It was sometimes hard to explain about the green smears on our arms and legs, and why our hands were so black. We tried to clean ourselves up with water from the old pump in the stable yard. Nanny used to grumble "I don't know how you can get yourselves so filthy when you've got all that lovely clean grass to play on"!

"Mops!, Fathead!" standing by the glass doors that separated the Nursery corridor from the Grown Ups landing,

Grandpa was calling us. Mary was 'Mops' because of her wild, curly hair. I don't know why I was 'Fathead', perhaps because of my round face. I liked having my leg pulled by Grandpa. His teasing never felt malicious. I liked being rescued from my sometimes over-serious 'Petre' self. He had a light touch. Grandpa in his sixties was of average height, slim with a tonsure of silver grey hair. He had a pencil thin moustache and was always spruce and well groomed. He wore Harris Tweed plus fours. He was great fun. He enjoyed our company in a way that made him seem quite different to our other relatives.

As we walked with him he'd suddenly say: "Stop! Listen". We heard rustlings in the undergrowth, wind in the trees, birds calling near at hand and far away. He taught us to recognise bird calls and to identify trees and wild flowers. He showed us how to look at the natural world and listen to it. He taught us to fish.

The Garden Pool was half way up the wooded hill that rose steeply on the south side of the park. You walked across the park, leaving the castle on your right. It was hard work for short legs toiling up the hill through the dense undergrowth and tormenting flies. Here you came suddenly upon a secret pool surrounded by trees and bracken. A long time ago it had been scooped out of the hillside to act as a small reservoir to catch the water of streams that ran down the hill. Pipes had been laid to carry the water down and across the park into the walled kitchen garden, a mile away. The pool, about 100 yards long, was well stocked with fish. Here grandpa practised casting with a fly. Every year our grandparents went up to Moffat in the Scottish Borders for the trout fishing.

On our first day we caught three perch – lovely little silver fish with red fins and tails. Cooked for breakfast next day they tasted, disappointingly, of mud.

While we were young we ate all our meals in the day nursery. The nurseries shared the floor with Uncle Eddie. His rooms were at the far end but occasionally he would come and stand silently near the glass doors that led to the Adults' world. He was very large and bulky with a full Edwardian beard. He looked like pictures of Edward VII. He was frightening because he never spoke a word. Mary called him "Uncle Eddie Wolf". Sometimes you would see him, in a fawn overcoat, walking very fast across the park with a walking stick, the butler several yards behind, having difficulty keeping up with his charge. I wonder about him, my unfortunate great uncle. Did he want to join the grown ups? Was he curious about these children that appeared on his floor once a year? I have no memory of his family members coming to see him. Where did he go when my grandparents left the house? He died in 1942.

While we were at A.B. there were a number of set annual expeditions. One was up the hill to the Shell House. This round stone house was like the beehive cells built by ancient hermits in Western Ireland. It was said to date from the time the Benedictines of Liege lodged at Acton Burnell in the 1770s as guests of Sir Edward Smythe, uncle of Maria Fitzherbert [1]. The stone house was decorated with shells and lined inside with Delft tiles and shells in patterns. There was a round stone table for picnics.

When Nanny felt affable she would walk us round the walled kitchen garden. She loved to eat the warm peaches growing against the red brick walls. There were bunches of grapes hanging down in the greenhouse and tomatoes growing in lines along the wall. She allowed us to pick and eat some fruit ourselves.

Another outing Nanny enjoyed, despite the steep climb, was going to tea with the head gamekeeper's wife. It was a two mile walk, all uphill towards the village of Ruckley. When small we thought we would never get there. At each bend in the lane there would be another hill ahead. At last, one more rise, and there was the cottage tucked into the hillside beside the woods. Mrs H. would be standing at her garden gate looking out for us. She and her husband had worked for the family all their lives.

Tea was laid out in the parlour. A wonderful spread of scones, sandwiches, cakes, chocolate biscuits, jelly, tinned peaches in a cut glass bowl. Nanny made you eat a mouthful of bread between each mouthful of delicious, golden, syrupy peach. It spoilt the peaches a bit, but not much.

One year when we were still small, Mary and I found our way, unseen, into the cool stone-flagged dairy. Great bowls of cream were waiting to be churned into butter. I found a basket of tomatoes.

"Let's throw the stalks into the cream!"

The green 'stars' made satisfying plops as they landed in the cream, they also made interesting patterns.

I forgot about the incident until the next summer when I overheard Mrs H laughing as she told our mother what she had found in her dairy after our last visit. Somehow

Nanny never got wind of this. I remember no dire repercussion.

After tea Mr H would come home with his gun and three dogs. The dogs were shut in their kennels and he took us up the path towards the wood, to show us his 'larder'. Suspended from a wire fence were rows of animal and bird carcasses in various stages of decay. Rooks, crows, magpies, jackdaws, hawks, foxes, weasels, stoats, rats – anything that might prey upon the precious pheasants and partridges. The putrefaction was horrible. Skulls without fur or feather, sharp teeth in skulls that were eyeless. They had all been punished and it made me feel sick. Going on to see the hens brooding on pheasant eggs or looking after fluffy chicks did not help.

But it was downhill all the way home.

Another expedition was made with the grown ups, not Nanny. There was a long walk across the park, pass the two lakes and a gothic hunting lodge on a knoll of trees, through wooden gates onto the lane. Along the lane you passed a farmyard wall with a row of cackling guinea fowl and then, at last, down a steep wooded bank to a cottage called Bull Hollow. It was a Hansel and Gretel house with wooden eaves, and lattice windows. It stood beside a tumbling stream. While the grown ups talked to the old couple we were free to explore the wood and the stream.

Our childhood world was filled with 'Do's' and 'Don'ts' but we also had a lot of time when no one knew what we were up to. No one worried that we would come to harm in woods and fields and streams. No one feared that we would break precious objects in the house. Were they totally unaware of where we were or what we might be doing? Were we, perhaps, trusted to behave properly? The insouciance of the grown ups may have added to my sense of responsibility for Mary, and certainly increased the dictums in my head about the need for sensible behaviour.

At Acton Burnell and Tor Bryan there were favourite outdoor spots for afternoon tea on summer days. At Tor Bryan this was on benches under a clump of bamboos by the pond. At Acton Burnell the family ranged itself in a line on deck chairs along the south side of the house looking towards the park. The house party was often joined by Grandpa's sister, Great Aunt Isabel, dressed in a floating silken dress and her companion, Miss Ward ('old Wardie') in her jacket, thick skirt and sensible brogues. Before this audience Mary was encouraged to do a few songs. Her clear rendering of George Formby's 'When I go Cleaning Windows' caused much laughter. It made me angry. The grown-ups were, in some way, 'taking the mickey'. I was probably very jealous of the attention she was getting.

This magical world ended in 1939.

That August we stayed at Acton Burnell for the last time in order to help with the packing up. I was thirteen and it was very hot. My first period came and this was a preoccupation for me amidst all the flurry of packing cases and worried adults. Our grandparents were moving out as they could no longer afford the upkeep and a London convent wanted to rent the house. Because of all the rumours about an impending war the removal date was brought forward. The grandparents were going to lodge with friends in Church Stretton. Some things were put into store; some were sold and no doubt a lot simply vanished. Amid the panic it was decided to send Mary and me home to Norfolk. We went to stay with Aunt Sheila at Langley Hall. I remember feeling very upset about this. Apparently we behaved badly as Daddy scolded me for giving trouble to our kind hostess when everyone was so preoccupied about the possibility of war.

Someone took us to Sunday Mass in Beccles. During the service the priest told us war had been declared. Immediately an air raid siren went off. I feared the worst.

---

[1] *The Catholic Families by Mark Bence-Jones, Constable, 1992, p.84*

Marjorie's Diary for 1941

The record for this year is kept in a very different diary from the book she used, ten years before, in 1931. Her life has changed as well.

This is an A5 black hardback book. It looks austere, befitting its appearance in the third year of the war. It is an Estate Book as well as a diary and is issued by the Country Gentleman's Association Limited. An initial line drawing shows a tractor ploughing a vast field with the heading "All the Year Round Farm by Fordson". There are advertisements for Water Softeners, Herald kitchen ranges, ladders, wire netting, gravel for drives, tennis balls and tennis courts. Quotations can be given for dredging waterways and for felling timber. There is information on income tax, sur-tax and death duties. There are recent amendments to the Emergency Laws passed subsequent to the outbreak of war. These measures include the Evacuation of Civil population, the requisition of premises and vehicles, the provision of water for extinguishing fire and the use of land for experiments with explosives.

These diary pages illustrate how hard it must have been for many, including my father, to conduct business.

The Ministry of Agriculture had, by now, very sweeping powers.

> *January 1ˢᵗ "Let's hope New Year brings Peace. We are so wonderfully quiet here."*

Did she believe that the war might end during 1941? She starts to record the books she is reading:

January

The Fall of France	*G.Waterfield*
Spring Returns	*D.Wallace*
The Long Week-end	*R.Graves*

February

The Last Days of Paris	*A.Werth*

Here, regrettably, her list ends.

Those Christmas holidays seem to have been fun for us children and probably for her as well.

> *January 2ⁿᵈ "We have a nice day in Norwich. Nanny lends me her car. Dr M finds Mary's eyes perfect, thanks be. We shop. Lunch at Princes and go to see film, Crazy Gang, at the Haymarket, and have tea. Ann and I saw Pride and Prejudice on Monday."*

> *January 3ʳᵈ Fetch Richard (13) and Christopher (11). R. not in uniform yet but has passed exams and goes to Dartmouth soon. We all go panto in the afternoon, Red Riding Hood, quite good and tea at the Haymarket. They are such nice boys (They are her friend Sib's children).*

January 5th Take children early Mass. Christopher wears Mary's coat. They snowball in the afternoon.

January 10th "Arranging house for the Ball. Go Norwich and fetch food. A Lovely evening. 8 grownups, 8 boys and 9 girls. Very nice party. Radiogram went all right.

I remember this event well. We were all aged between eleven and sixteen. The drawing room was cleared of furniture for dancing. I thought Heron Dixon, the eldest boy, dashing in his kilt!

The following week it was very cold and snowy and everyone got bad colds.

January 20th "A sad morning, snowy and horrid. They get away at 9 am with hot bottles and rugs"

Albert drove us through the snow to Newnam Paddox school. Mary was sick on the way. Once there the car got stuck in the snow by the drive gates, so in thin shoes and coats, Mary and I walked a mile through snow to reach the school. Albert was put up at the lodge gate and had a very bad journey back to Norfolk the next day.

It seems to have been a harsh winter. The diary speaks of it being exceedingly cold. There are several bouts of snow. Helen is often very often ill. Marjorie does a lot of sewing for the Red Cross. Albert joins the RAF and is moved about the country. On March 1st they get 5 lbs of tea and 20 lbs of sugar from William's brother, Bernard, in Calcutta. (The weekly ration was 55 g of tea and 225 g of sugar.)

By March 10th the weather was improving and Marjorie set out with a friend to visit us at school.

"We have a very successful trip on a lovely sunny day. We lunch in Huntingdon and get to the convent at 4.45 pm Take children to the pub where we have a good tea. I walk them back to the house and see the Nun (the head). Walk back to the village for supper with M. Nice fire in the sitting room and oil stove in our bedroom. Sleep with rugs and coats all over us."

The next day they take the girls into Rugby. Ann gets nice new shoes for 23/-. They go to see Deanna Durbin in 'Spring Parade' after a good lunch at the George.

"Ann not quite perfect. Doesn't get on with the Head nun"

She starts getting troubled with bad headaches and an old sensation of smelling wood smoke she arranges to go and see her osteopath in Birmingham.

"Hope we shan't have any bombs".

Before she leaves, Guelder, our Dutch Keeshond dog:

"kills one of my beauty cockies. He's getting to be a villain. Steals food and is all naughtiness."

She went by train to Birmingham and found the guest house:

"very dismal – over 60 windows broken when a bomb fell in December. Broken windows all covered up black. So

many gaps in houses. A siren moans at 10.30 pm but I fall asleep and do not hear All Clear at 11.15 pm."

After three treatments she goes by train up to Shropshire to visit her parents at Church Stretton. On her return journey the train is delayed and takes over three hours to reach Paddington. But a taxi speeds her across to Liverpool Street to catch the 3.40 pm to Norwich.

The diary shows that travel in England in 1941 was possible provided you had enough petrol coupons or income for train fares. There were also opportunities to eat out in cafes and hotels. The cinema and theatre were great sources of relaxation.

On March 28th she records various bombs in the distance and in a few days they go to see huge craters on Langley marsh and in a local field. The Easter holidays start and she buys a pony trap and harness. We have two ponies who take turns in pulling the trap. We made an expedition to see the enormous crater made by a dropped land mine near a wooded pool called Hellesmere Hole. One day:

"W rings up to say not to go to Norwich as Colman's (mustard factory) badly burnt last night and an unexploded bomb near the Carrow Road."

My father organised the Royal Observer Corps Lookout Post in a wooden hut near a pill box, on a slight rise, outside Loddon above the Beccles road. He would get information about aircraft, bombs and casualties in the area.

We returned to school at the end of April. She writes:

"Am sad, Ann and I rather naggy during holidays."

At fifteen I am probably a fairly self-opinionated young teenager. I think our mother missed the buzz of the holidays.

On May 9th she went with a friend to see Richard Tauber in 'The Land of Smiles'.

"He is magnificent. He nurses his voice rather and not full volume but very fine. Chinese make-up v. good but he is very ugly!"

I admire her resourcefulness in using the pony trap to visit friends. One day she does a round trip of about twenty miles. On another day:

"Nice walk to see the crater and pick cowslips in the park. Helen roars a good deal when she doesn't get her own way."

She seems to be a cheeky little toddler calling her parents 'Daddy Petar' and 'Mummy Petar'.

"Helen is very clever. I show her a cartoon in the Daily Mail of Hitler on a horse.' Bad Hitler, I no like.' She seems to know his face anywhere." Nanny has been away for a week. *"I wonder why Helen is so 'nasty' once Nanny is back. Says 'go away' and yet is so loving and amiable when I'm in charge."*

June 1st "What a bombshell! Clothes to be rationed. 66 coupons a year...Crete has been evacuated."

In June my father and mother visit us at school. I'm unhappy and depressed and want to leave. *"William gets her to see she must be plucky and stay on."* I wonder how threatening the war news was at this time. Is that why they visited us? Is that why I was so unsettled?

The weather is very hot all June and July. Grandpa has been getting ill. On July 23rd the friend our grandparents are staying with near Church Stretton, rings my mother to say she feels my grandmother needs someone with her. *"Such a shock and just when the children are returning".* In the Shrewsbury nursing home next day she learns that he has a malignant growth on his lung. *"He looks ghastly. Hardly knows me."* A second medical opinion confirms that he has no hope of recovery. My mother stays in Shropshire and on August 8th Mary and I go to join her. Grandpa is moved after a while into another friend's house in Church Stretton in sight of his beloved hills. I remember being shocked at his appearance when we visited him. My mother and her sister Mariel look after their mother and it is arranged that Mary and I can hire ponies and ride on the Long Mynd.

It became for Mary and me an unforgettable summer. There was the background sadness of our grandfather's illness and the worried preoccupation of the grown ups, but there was also the freedom of days spent riding on the upland moors.

"August 18th. Ann and M go for a ride and get back late"
– underlined three times

This was the day as I remember it. On top of the Long

Mynd we decided to take a short cut back to our farm-house. It was already dusk when we started our descent at the head of a valley. We followed the stream. Mary led the way. Her pony, Pip, was nimble and sure-footed. My larger cob, Chesterfield, was clumsy. We slithered over wet boulders moving from one side of the falling water, to the other. Suddenly Chesterfield half fell. Suppose we came to a really steep drop with a waterfall. What if my cob broke a leg? It was getting too late and dark to retrace our steps to the high moors.

"Will we be alright, Ann?"

"Yes, the valley will widen out soon" I prayed.

It was almost dark. Suddenly Pip stopped.

"I can't see the way anymore!"

"Let the reins go slack, he'll find his way. He'll be hungry and want to get home"

It worked. We moved forward again. I could just see Pip's dappled flanks in the gloom.

Gradually the stream fell less steeply and a path emerged. The ponies leapt out of the freezing water onto the bank. Ahead the light of a cottage glimmered. We were down!

As we neared our farm dark shapes appeared. Our mother had persuaded a few locals to come looking for us. She was in tears. Once again I had been the irresponsible older sister and worried the grown ups. Ah! Me!

Mary and I returned to Norfolk. A week later our mother followed us.

"Say 'Au Revoir' to the poor old chap. So sad to leave him."

She sees William, Ann and Helen who came to meet her at Norwich station.

"How big my lamb has got and hair lovelier than ever. Sits on my knee all way home quite surprised to see 'Mummee'".

Helen has not seen her for 6 weeks.

On September 8th she gets a telegram. Grandpa has died. She returns immediately to Shropshire and my dad follows the next day for the funeral. I feel very upset that no asks me I whether I want to go. While they are away the head gardener at Langley Hall dies. My mother returns too exhausted to face a second funeral so I am given the honour of escorting my father to Hardley church for Mr Bentley's funeral. It is the first funeral I go to. I wish it was my grandfather's…

My mother wrote about her father's funeral in the chapel at Acton Burnell.

"A lovely requiem sung by the sweet nuns who did it all so beautifully. I hold Mum's dear hand and try to comfort her. The bearers are Tipton, Howlett, Stockton, Old Mac, Rowlands, and Tom Morgan.

(Possibly the men who had carried hayforks at her wedding sixteen years earlier.)

Before going back to school we celebrated her birthday a few days early, by taking the pony trap and riding the ponies across the park to Bullfinch Glade to pick blackberries.

II

Oxford

1944 – 1947

I soon realised that Oxford would be even more fun if I had a boyfriend. Not to sleep with, of course, but as a handy partner for college dances, concerts, events. Lots of boring girls had steady boyfriends, some of them really good-looking. Unfortunately the men I fancied usually seemed destined for the priesthood, or had a girl friend back home.

In my third term I met Cecil Bellarmine. He was a well known figure and I was immensely flattered when he began to take an interest. He was older, having been invalided out of the Navy. He was rather short and stout with a bullet shaped head, but he had dynamism. He had a rich, plummy voice and his oratory in debates had immense emotional appeal. Much later, it emerged, that a lot of women had gone out with Cecil. I was the last of a long line.

Cecil knew everybody. He took me everywhere. He was very masterful and a bit odd. It was exciting to be seen out with an older man. My friends in college began to worry about me. If Cecil told me to miss a lecture or a tutorial, I did. Despite his 'help' my fortnightly essays got skimpier.

It was a college ruling that we all had to do some 'voluntary' war work. This might be serving in the government subsidised British Restaurant, cleaning in the Radcliffe Infirmary, gardening or other jobs for the college. My job was to deliver mail between the colleges. I was provided with a very large satchel.

One day, delivering mail to Cecil's college I met him in the porter's lodge.

"Come and have some tea in my rooms."

It was the first time he had invited me to do this.

"I have to deliver these letters."

"You can do that later. It's cold. Come and get warm with a cup of tea first".

He took me by the hand – he had pudgy, rather sticky hands – and led me to his ground floor room overlooking Garden Quad.

There were crumpets with golden syrup and the inevitable chocolate cake from the cake factory in the Banbury Road. It was warm in his room and it was pouring outside.

"I should deliver those letters."

"Don't worry, Ann. You are such a worry-bunny. Come and sit beside me. I've got a friend who'll deliver them for you. Give me the bag and forget all about them. I want to stroke your lovely hair."

Sometime later he said:

"For being a good girl I'm going to take you out to dinner at the Randolph."

Sometime later, after a very good meal and a brandy, he said:

"I want you to show me that you trust me completely. There's a place I know where we can climb into college. I want you to sleep in my bedroom, up on the third floor. I shall sleep on the sofa in my sitting room. Will you do that, Ann?"

I did not like the idea at all. My face showed this. He now sounded angry:

"Our relationship will go nowhere, Ann, unless you trust me implicitly. You do, don't you?"

The rain had stopped. We went over a disused railway siding, through an empty engine shed and up a high brick wall. Here there were foot holes and someone had cut back the barbed wire on the top of the wall. Now it was a jump down onto a shed and we were in garden quad.

I hated going to bed without washing. Cecil said not to risk being seen by going to the bathroom. His bedroom was icy cold. I hardly slept. At six am he came to see me back over the wall.

I didn't see Cecil for several days. One lunchtime there was a note in my pigeonhole from the Assistant Bursar, saying she needed to see me urgently. Puzzled I went to her office. The Principal Bursar was also there. Two tall, middle aged women in Harris tweed suits.

"Ann Petre, what is the meaning of this?" One of them held out a satchel.

"This bag with your number on was found in Winchester College, full of undelivered mail...We have had tutors, college porters, even the Dean of Christchurch, ringing to ask about missing documents...Can you explain what happened?"

I remember the hot shame, but I do not remember what explanation I gave. The punishment was dreadful. I had to apologise for every delayed missive– to college porters, to dons all over North Oxford. It took two days before the bag was empty. I was demoted from messenger to mucking out the rabbits on the college allotment. The smell of manure still reminds me of the bursar's office.

Of course, Cecil laughed it all off.

"Those ridiculous old women with nothing better to worry about than a few unimportant notes. The significant thing that has come out of this is you getting to trust me more...Trust between us is everything...You felt quite safe in my bed didn't you? You can trust me my lovely Ann, always..."

He caressed my breasts.

"Can't you?...next term I want you to sleep in my bedroom again...or, I might climb into Saxmundham and sleep in yours..."

Next term came after the long summer vac. I had a great summer going to a National Union of Students summer camp. We picked peas on a farm in Worcestershire and I met a lovely chap from Manchester who wanted to become a Catholic. We had great talks walking round cornfields in the evening. I had the occasional rather weird letter from Cecil who had gone on a long retreat to an Anglican Priory in Devonshire. In his latest letter he wrote: "we need to make the ultimate sacrifice next term". I wondered what he meant.

As a second year undergraduate I moved out of college into digs up the Banbury Road. I had an attic room in a tall red brick house belonging to the three elderly sisters, the Misses Woolley. They received me for tea in their cluttered drawing room. They told me I could have male visitors from 2-4 pm. I knew this would annoy Cecil.

He called on the first day of term having got my address from the college lodge. His hands and face were very cold although it was a warm October day. He looked pale and strained. His cheeks were puffy and his breath smelt awful.

"Dearest Ann!" he fell on his knees, and, grasping my wrist, pulled me down beside him.

"This is the feast day of our Holy Guardian Angels, and the day appointed for the ultimate sacrifice."

He held both my hands in his.

"I want you to remain kneeling while I give you the Angels' blessing."

He stood up and laid his now sweaty palms on my head. He intoned a verse from the Latin Mass.

"Introibo ad altare Dei" …(I will go into the temple of the Lord.)

He began to press down, gently at first, then harder.

"Cecil...please...you're..."

His hands slipped down round my throat. He began to squeeze.

"The next part takes place on your bed..."

He started dragging me across the room.

"Cecil, please. I need to go to the bathroom..."

It worked. I had taken him by surprise.

"Come straight back..."

Shaking all over I went very quietly down the two flights of stairs, through the hall, out into the garden. I grabbed my bike and rode as fast as I could to Maximus College. I needed a rescuer and I thought Larry, a good friend and a medical student, would be the best person. I prayed he'd be in college. As it happened he was in the porter's lodge, on his way out.

"Oh! Larry, I need help...Cecil tried to strangle me, he's..."

"It's o.k. Ann. Where is he?"

"I left him in my new digs at the top of 228 Banbury Road"

"I'll go at once...you go back to college. I'll look for you later in the J.C.R."

Much later, Larry told me he had found my landladies in a state of great distress. Cecil was making a lot of noise in the attic and every now and again throwing furniture, china, my books, out of the window. There was a pile in the garden below.

Two policemen arrived and Larry went with them upstairs. Cecil had barricaded himself in my room with a chest of drawers. He shouted at them to go away and find Ann as she was in a very bad state. Eventually they got into the room. Larry talked to Cecil and Cecil agreed to go to the police station to make a statement about Ann. On the way to the station, Larry said, Cecil thought he saw me and tried to get out of the car. He became wild and abusive and had to be restrained.

Cecil was taken to a psychiatric hospital and sectioned. Larry told me he had had a breakdown before.

The principal decided that I should spend the rest of the year back in college. My friends were relieved that things had got back to normal. I began acting in the Experimental Theatre Club with the likes of Ken Tynan, Derek Hart and Keith Dewhurst.

Later I became an enthusiastic member and secretary of the Union of Catholic Students. In the presence of Cardinal Griffin in the Westminster Cathedral Hall I delivered a rousing speech to the assembled students:

"We are all called to be Saints!"

Lately, on a trip to Assisi, I met a woman I had not seen since those heady days.

"You were a very keen Roman Catholic. As a rather vague Anglican I was impressed!"

Notting Hill Gate

1947 – 1949

What to do after Oxford? The Principal of my college tried to get me a fellowship of a US College. I was keen to continue studying as I was not sure what else to do. My outline scheme of putative research was about the links between psychology – or was it philosophy – and physiology. I was awarded a *proxime accessit* – the academic phrase for 'runner up'.

The Principal was trustee of prestigious institutes. She got me a job in central London. She was generous with her time and helped her young graduates. I also believed that my father had charmed her. My new employers did not have a position for a graduate in P.P.E. with no research experience. My manager said, on my first day,

"Frankly I don't know what to do with you. You are useless to us without secretarial skills. I advise you to enrol at once in an evening class". It was plain that I had been foisted on the institute.

Dejectedly I went to Pitman classes in Southampton Row. I struggled with typing and shorthand. After a few months the institute developed a new grant awarding branch. It was decided to move me into it.

I now worked with a charming young man sorting out the paperwork for grants for old people's projects. I occasionally went to visit an old people's home to vet its application. But mostly I moved coloured flags on a map and assembled wads of paper for the governors' meetings. Lady Sybil, one of the governors, knew my family in Norfolk. I think she led my father to believe I was achieving great things. Truth was, I was bored to death. I felt there must be more to life than this. I was getting nowhere with my goal of 'working for poor people'.

I lodged in Linden Gardens near Notting Hill Gate underground station. I soon grew to loathe strap-hanging on the Central line. The house belonged to a foreign brother and sister who had fled the continent before the war.

The room had a huge, draughty window looking into the boughs of a lime tree. There were no curtains and the shadows of the branches moved endlessly, by the light of a street lamp, on the wall beside my bed. My bedding was a palliasse made of coarse white cotton stuffed with straw like we used when I went to guide camp years before. It was prickly and gave no warmth. I cooked on a small gas ring. There was a microscopic gas fire. An aunt came to see me.

"This tea is delicious, it has a biscuity flavour".

I was out of milk and, remembering this, had poured the surplus off my morning cornflakes.

My social life was at a very low ebb. I saw an aunt and uncle in Ebury Street and a mannered young man who had just started at the Foreign Office. At weekends I read 'War and Peace', walked in the Parks, practised my shorthand – I had no typewriter – and went to Mass at the Carmelite Priory in Church Street.

What had become of all my Oxford friends? We had dispersed. Bill was in articles in Birmingham and visited occasionally. There were drinks with acquaintances in 'The Bunch of Grapes' after High Mass in the oratory. Tim was in Brussels.

My attitude to men was ambivalent. I lived in a world described so well by David Lodge in "How far can you go?" [1] I was a sensual young woman and I wanted sex in the undefined way a Catholic girl of my generation was likely to want it. That is, lovely, fulfilling sex within marriage as described by my mother. The other pull I experienced was towards sacrifice. That voice urged ultimate self denial by leading a life of chastity, and of total dedication to the service of God and poor people. It was a voice familiar to my seven year old self onwards. The voice had spoken to me before I left Oxford. Painfully, in my third year, for reasons I didn't understand, I ended a relationship with a man I loved, for the sake of some vague 'ideal'. He had been baffled and deeply hurt. At one level, for me, it had something to do with his not being a Catholic.

At another level it may have been my deep suspicion about personal happiness. What I desired could seem to be morally dangerous. Life was somehow safer if it hurt.

A few months into my life in London these conflicting feelings clashed once more.

"Zair iss a telephone call for you, Mees Petre...Please do not talk long. My bruzzer iss awaiting a call..."

I was rarely telephoned. The Wolfes grudgingly allowed the occasional incoming call from my parents. Mr Wolfe was an art dealer and the upright black telephone, with separate ear piece, stood surrounded by Chinese bowls and willow pattern plates. The Wolfes always remained in the room. I was too inhibited by their disapproving presence to say much.

"Hello", a man's voice.

"My aunt met your mother at an old girls reunion last week. They hatched a plot that we should meet"

"Oh! Yes, my mother wrote about that in a letter I got this morning." He sounded nice.

"Shall we fall in with their scheming and meet? Some friends and I are going to a restaurant on the Thames next Saturday evening. Would you like to join us?"

Miss Wolfe dropped something and I felt I must hurry.

"Yes, yes, I'd like that very much."

"My aunt gave me your address... shall I pick you up at seven?"

"Yes, that would be fine."

"I look forward to meeting you"

His voice sounded as if he was smiling. Miss Wolfe advanced towards me.

"Me too!"

I rang off. Miss Wolfe glared as I fled back to my room that for once looked a bit more welcoming. I spent the rest of the evening deciding what I would wear.

He came a week later, at seven pm, in a taxi. I was waiting outside under the portico. He was tall and very good looking with brown eyes. He smiled as he held out a hand to help me in. He was friendly, easy to talk to. His friends at the restaurant were a slightly older couple, also easy to get to know. The food was excellent. It was the best evening I'd had since Oxford.

A month later I got an invitation to go on a residential weekend to study the New Testament at a retreat house run by a new Catholic organisation called the Crucible. I first came across the Crucible at Oxford. I knew some thought it very unorthodox. A young man friend said:

"I think it's a cheat to dress up as an attractive young woman when you are really a disguised nun."

A friend introduced me to the head of Crucible. I found her formidable. I got the impression, from the outset, that she saw me as a desirable recruit. My early difficulties with my father and bossy nanny made me wary of physically large, powerful people, especially women. I resented feeling controlled, but could find it hard, in some situations, not to appear subservient or passive.

Now It was Whitsun. The old farmhouse with a rambling garden was among fields at the end of the Bakerloo line. The villages around still had signs of their rural past. On the Saturday morning I was woken early by the cuckoo. I dressed, went outdoors and walked to the end of the lane. I had forgotten the smell of a May morning, the sense of being re-born into a perfect world.

The cuckoo was circling a small larch wood, its persistent call now close, now far away. Other birds were singing. A lark went up from a field nearby. Under the trees were waves of bluebells. A bee bumbled into me. The sun grew warmer. A woodpecker was hard at work.

I sat on a log and thought about him. We'd met three times, and each time it grew better. He was companionable. I was enjoying life again; there were things to look forward to. I really liked him but I was beginning to have feelings like those that had swamped me at Oxford when men kissed me. "Should I do this? I like it so much…am I leading him on? How far can I go? What am I meant to do? What's God's will for me?" Initial certainty and happiness would give way to doubt, confusion, and hesitancy. Now it was all starting up again. What was I to do?

Last night the leader of the Crucible had asked me to consider joining them full-time.

"We are a pioneering organisation in the Catholic Church. We need people like you…well educated, with a developed sense of the spiritual life…You seem to me, since we last talked in Oxford, to have a greater desire to dedicate yourself to others…I feel you are not altogether happy with your life at present?"

I reflected that a very eminent woman was taking me seriously. A woman in her forties, she had come to England, from the continent to found a branch of The Crucible in this country. Catholicism was more progressive where she came from than in England. The Crucible was a lay organisation, called, at that time, a secular institute. Members of its inner core, called Bearers were not nuns but after five years of training they could take simple vows or promises of poverty, chastity and obedience. They ran the farmhouse where I was staying. They organised study days, retreats, and prayer meetings. They had a number of publications. Some went out to work.

The Crucible staff running the weekend seemed friendly happy young women. They were a talented group. They told me they were planning a big event in the Royal Albert Hall. The aim was to tell people about the life of Christ and put The Crucible in the limelight in the hopes of attracting new members. Would I like to sell some tickets?

Taking the train back to the Big Smoke on Whit Sunday evening was a huge anti climax. It hurt to leave the woods and fields on a glorious May evening. It was getting dark by the time I emerged at Notting Hill Gate. My room was cold and lonely. Tomorrow would be a day of unrewarding work, an evening class and baked beans for supper. The companionship of the Crucible beckoned.

What about the young man I had met that spring? He dropped out of my life as I became more involved with the

Crucible. He reappeared later when he married someone I knew well.

⁽¹⁾ *How far can you go? David Lodge, Penguin, 1980, page 31*

  "Dennis got his hand inside Angela's blouse and on to a brassiere cup. Then there was a setback. One day Angela emerged weeping from the confessional...and for a long time there was no touching of legs or breast in any circumstances."

The Crucible

1949 – 1953

"Why can't you join a proper religious order?" *Father*

"Don't play with fire!" *Nun Friend*

"If you join the Crucible you can't ever come back"
Father

"It's crystal clear where your vocation lies".
Priest Adviser to the Crucible

"Did you have to do this to us?" *Mother*

"Don't ever leave me" *Helen, aged 10*

"Will you come home for Christmas?" *Mary, aged 20*

"We wish you all the best!" *Boss*

"Are you sure, Ann?" *Oxford Friend*

I worked out my notice at the office and went home to
Norfolk. My mother paid for us to have a farewell weekend
together in Cambridge – just she and me. We stayed at the
Garden House Hotel, a modest family hotel in those days.
Late February: sunlight slanting on pussy willows, catkins
bobbing in college gardens above aconites and crocuses.
Evensong in King's College Chapel on Ash Wednesday:

111

the Allegri Miserere – treble notes mounting, pausing on the cusp, falling like the flowers of lily of the valley. The bittersweet of Lent. A sharp wind blowing through the college courts.

"It's a disgrace" they said when I arrived at the Crucible farm in the middle of Lent. They were referring to my dowry and they were looking at what I had brought from my London digs in a hired lorry – an old iron bedstead, an antique clock from my Petre grandmother, all my books from Oxford. My father had refused to give me a penny. Years later a reader in the library at the Crucible was surprised to find Keynes and Kant on the shelves.

There were six of us novices. All in our twenties and from very different backgrounds. Two had been factory workers in the Midlands, two were Oxbridge graduates, and one girl had never worked. We slept in wooden huts dotted round the grounds. At six am the novice mistress banged on your door, "Benedicite". You answered "Deo Gratias", tumbled out of the wooden bunk, washed perfunctorily in freezing water, dressed and went to the chapel for mental prayer and Mass. Sometimes the full moon shone through the sweetcorn outside my hut.

The first six months were spent in hard manual labour and in learning how to meditate. I scrubbed mud laden artichokes, dug up vegetables from half-frozen ground, polished floors, and learnt to cook at speed for a community of twenty. In my nervousness as assistant sacristan, I dropped the sanctuary lamp so that its oil spilt all down a pristine wall. In the kitchen I broke more china than anyone before. It was all incredibly exhausting but also satisfying. For parts of some days I knew an inner peace that surpassed all understanding. My problems were physical. Onions and other root vegetables and rough wholemeal bread gave me indigestion.

Rehearsals started for the Albert Hall Play. Another novice and I were in charge of the box office. I was also an assistant producer. Large groups of Crucible members came in bus loads from all parts of the country.

On the day of the final dress rehearsal, I went to get my hair set at inexpensive hairdressers in Hammersmith. We were meant to look neat and well groomed. The hairdresser ran late and by the time I got out it was five-thirty The rehearsal was due to start at six. There was a jostling crowd at the bus stop but I managed to squeeze on a bus. It was five-forty I should just make it. After a few minutes a lot of people got off and to my horror I realised the bus was heading west down King's Road, away from my destination. I had caught the wrong bus. By the time I got the right bus and reached the Albert Hall it was six-forty and the rehearsal was in full swing. The producer was extremely annoyed with me. She was starting flu and losing her voice. I did my best to direct the crowd scenes. The rehearsal went well.

The play ran for three days. The tickets all sold out. It was very well reviewed and the Cardinal congratulated the Crucible movement. We were on the map. The Crucible had arrived.

A week later I was summoned from my favourite corner

in the old greenhouse where I was scrubbing potatoes. The novice mistress looked grim.

"The Superior wants to see you in her room."

She only saw us novices on the gravest of occasions. Last time, someone's father had died.

I knocked on her door. She was very angry. I trembled.

"D. has had to go back to bed. She has a secondary ear infection from the flu. I have only just heard how you let her down by arriving very late for the dress rehearsal. This is a serious matter. What is your excuse?"

"I…I caught a bus going the wrong way…"

She looked even angrier and raised her arm as if to strike. I cowered.

"That is a most ridiculous and pathetic excuse…you with your Oxford degree caught the wrong bus…it's impossible. Ann, what were you doing?"

I couldn't think of anything to say, except

"I caught the right bus going the wrong way."

She moved as if to shake me but then flung away towards the window.

I had flashbacks to the bathroom with my father, to school with the headmistress…

She cleared her throat.

"To be on time is an essential aspect of religious obedience. Your act of gross disobedience must be severely punished…I am about to send the other novices for a week's break to the Scilly Isles. You will stay here and help J. pick nettles. She will teach you to make nettle soup…we drink a lot of nettle soup…So far, Ann, you have been a pretty useless candidate for the Crucible. You'll have to change a lot if you are ever to become a Bearer."

Years later, in therapy, I dreamt:

"I am back in her panelled room. I see it's really a very large coffin. She suddenly picks me up by the legs and I turn into a floor mop. She dips my head in a bucket of filthy water and uses me to wash the walls of the coffin…"

About a year later I was summoned again.

"Your father, Ann, has been very kind lately advising me on what we might do with the three fields we have just been given. He tells me that he and your mother will be celebrating their silver wedding in the summer. I have decided to give you permission to attend the celebration."

I heard this with mixed feelings. I was glad that the superior and my father were getting on better. I was not sure that I wanted to go back to Norfolk for a celebration dinner dance.

Miss Leman our village dressmaker made me an evening top and skirt for the dance. There was a marquee on the front lawn and friends came from all over Norfolk, and beyond. As I had expected they didn't know how to deal with me. I felt unhappy and out of place. I danced a few times with my father and a few times with Helen. Mary looked radiant in a wonderful dress. At the end of the evening she announced her engagement.

The day after I got back the novice mistress said:

"About this trouble you've been having with your digestion. I've decided you'd better sleep in the house. The garden may be too damp for you."

One of the great consolations of the life had been the peace of my hut. I could hear the birds and watch the changing skies. No one lived near. On an occasional Quiet Day we could spend a whole day in our huts, reading, writing, praying, even sketching. The huts got very snug as we were each allowed a paraffin stove.

Indoors I was given a room to share with two new novices. I've always been a light sleeper. One of the girls snored. Our room was next to the bathroom on an echoing corridor. Among my new troubles sleep deprivation was the worst.

I was worried about my father. At the time of the Silver Wedding he had confided that he wasn't feeling well. Soon after, a specialist said he had hardening of the arteries and high blood pressure.

"I've seen the red light" he said. I did not know what he meant exactly, and I felt unable to ask. Since I had joined the Crucible he had seemed even more depressed and withdrawn than before. I was sure my choice of future had made him ill. It was a frightening thought. Somehow I had to make a success of my chosen life.

Time passed, we went on pilgrimage to Rome and were

blessed by Pope Pius XII. We made the return journey by train and some of us slept on the carriage floor. Then the six of us, including my best friend H. were sent to work in the London house. My job was to help with Crucible publications. I went out to speak to schools and youth clubs all over London. One Advent two of us were sent to a northern diocese to organise groups to sell Christmas cards 'on the knocker' with the aim "To put Christ back into Christmas." In a filthy tenement I watched a mother feed her eight small children by pouring a can of baked beans onto a box. The children devoured the beans with their fingers. I had not known such poverty existed.

One summer after I had been with the Crucible four years the novice mistress said to H. and me:

"You've worked hard this year. Here's four pounds each, you can go anywhere – but be back in ten days time."

Early next day we were on the M1 heading north. We wanted to get to Skye. The couple who stopped had a large fast car. They dropped us near Glasgow. A second lift took us to Arisaig. A woman in a cottage let us a room with a brass bedstead and a lumpy mattress. She agreed to give us a cooked breakfast and sandwiches. She told us where we could hire bicycles.

Loch Morar had a small chapel by the water. An old priest said Mass each morning. The sun shone on a wide sandy beach. Gulls screamed overhead.

At Mallaig we looked across a rough sea to the Cuillins shrouded in mist. We had not got enough money for the ferry to Skye.

117

The day we headed south it poured all day. Lifts were few. I did not have a waterproof and my tweed coat got soaked. H made a telephone call to cousins near Kendal. They put us up for the night and set us on our road. We had to get home that day.

A car stopped. A miracle! It was the couple who had given us our first lift ten days before. They had cut their holiday short because of the relentless rain. They took us almost all the way. We walked into the kitchen at ten pm I was feeling unwell.

A week later I had pneumonia. A complementary therapist was consulted. She recommended that I be wrapped in thermogene. This was orange coloured wadding impregnated with anti-inflammatory poultice. With three hot bottles I was put to bed for 'the heat cure'. I burned and sweated for a week. My temperature came down and I was allowed up. I felt extremely weak and for the next few weeks I had a succession of colds. I also had indigestion and heartburn most of the time. I had lost quite a lot of weight.

My mother wrote to say my father was ill and she was at her wits end.

The superior said:

"We are aware that you have a lot of health and family problems. We have consulted Father Dominic. We have decided, after due deliberation, that you are not fitted for Crucible life. We believe that you should go home and help your parents."

I listened to this with a sense of disbelief. I knew things weren't good but I had not expected a summary dismissal.

I felt a complete failure. I had not achieved what I had set out to do. I felt rejected and humiliated.

"Father Dominic would like to talk to you. We would prefer that you did not speak to anyone else. Get your things together and one of us will give you a lift to the station after breakfast."

Father Dominic was kind. I had always liked him. I wept. He helped me decide that I needed a few days before going to Norfolk. He suggested that I asked Mary if I could stay with her in London. As I got up to go he said:

"Never forget, Ann, that what you have learned here will be with you for the rest of your life."

Norfolk 1954

My bedroom door burst open. My clock read three am

"Ann come quickly...Daddy...he's collapsed."

My father was lying half on, half off their bed, groaning, twitching and now vomiting everywhere.

"Mummy, go and telephone Dr B...Call Marion (the maid) and get her to come and help us."

With great difficulty the three of us got him onto the bed and removed the soiled linen. All the time he resisted, cursing and swearing in blurred tones.

"Leave me alone. You damned women..."

He thrashed about knocking things off the bedside table.

"Get me Albert..."

"Daddy, Dr B is coming. You aren't well. He'll make you more comfortable...we'll get Albert in the morning."

Suddenly he quietened. He lay quite still, his face and hands cold and sweaty. Marion took away the dirty linen.

"It was my fault," she whispered brokenly, "He was on top of me, he was trying...poor man...he was trying..." tears overwhelmed her. She was unable to go on. We both heard the sound of the doctor's car.

※ ·→ ═◉ ◉═ ·← ※

It was an hour later.

"I think he has had a cerebral haemorrhage. I've given him a sedative. He should sleep for a few hours. You need to get some rest, Mrs Petre...could you go into the spare room? Ann, could you rest in the dressing room with the door open...I'll get the nurse to come up in the morning and I'll ring Mr H and see if he will do a domiciliary as William is his patient...I'll be back later in the morning."

So began our nightmare. I had been home six weeks from The Crucible. I had a stomach ulcer and was on a restricted diet. I had been told to rest.

After that first night my father had two more strokes. It was difficult for him to walk. He became incontinent and lost his reason and most of his ability to speak. He was constantly agitated, wanting to get to his office in the village. Left on his own he would immediately drag himself to the front door. He fell trying to cross the garden and cut his head.

All his life he had been driven by what he saw as his duty. He was probably a workaholic, highly conscientious.

With his reason gone, the driving principle that remained in him seemed to be 'I must attend to my work'. Anyone who stood in his way met with his fury. He seemed to see my mother and I as his principal gaolers and the full force of his frustration and aggression was unleashed on us. He cursed and swore at us most of the time. This was devastating, particularly for my mother. It hampered the tasks of washing and feeding him and getting him onto the commode. We had to employ two part time nurses. He treated these women with more respect. The one person he positively enjoyed having with him was Albert.

"How are you today, Sir?"

"Oh! Not...so... good..."

"Would you like me to sit with you, Sir?"

"Yes..." rubbing his chin..."need...need...rough..."

"You'd like me to help you shave, Sir?"

"Yes...I...would..."

They went through this routine every morning. Albert had very limited sight as a result of the malnutrition he had suffered in the war, in Burma. But he managed to shave his employer skilfully, and with great gentleness. He talked while he did this.

"I'll be starting to plant up the long border, today, Sir... it was to be a mix of dianthus and salvia, at the front, wasn't it, Sir?...And then sweet scented stocks, asters and bergamot...and then, of course, we'll have the dahlias at the back..."

"Yes…yes…that sounds…"

"Perhaps you'd like me to walk with you later today, Sir…and show you how I've been getting on?"

"Yes…yes…thank you…Al…bert…"

Albert would help him dress and would settle him in his armchair.

"Times please…Al…"

He couldn't read anymore, but this fetching of the newspaper and getting his spectacles was part of the morning ritual.

Always a small, trim man, Albert's wartime experience as a prisoner of the Japanese, seemed to have shrunk him. But his small stature was more than compensated for by his depth of spirit. This was a man, who, his wife heard from former RAF colleagues, kept them alive in appalling conditions. These men were made to work hacking coral to build the infamous Burmese railroad. They had inadequate food and fell ill with fevers, including beri-beri. Men wanted to die but Albert would try to keep hope alive, He would tell them about Norfolk and the life he knew there at Langley Hall Farm.

"He'd tell us how Miss Mary would make jumps for the ponies. Then when Miss Ann had finished her lessons they'd be off on the ponies. Mary on the little Greymoth and Ann on the bigger, black one, Gypsy. Off they'd gallop through the woods, whooping and hollering like cowboys…Another time he told us how he went to work for the Captain when he was twelve. Captain Petre said he'd teach Alfie how to drive. He sat him in the driver's seat, showed him the gears, and told him to drive them up the Back Lane. Captain cursed every time he got a gear wrong. He was that frightened he learnt to drive in a day!"

Albert did the same for my mother and me. With persistence and gentle humour, he normalised what was otherwise nightmarish. The three of us were dealing, each in their own way, with the shocking loss of someone we admired and looked up to. Albert, throughout, remained devoted to the shambling wreck of a man who had been his ideal. He continued, to the end, to treat him with respect and gentleness.

Albert's life had been fundamentally altered by the war. When he got back from Burma in 1946 my father offered him his old job back. With a small injury pension he worked slightly shorter hours. He had very little sight as a result of the malnutrition and all he had been through, including having his appendix out without an anaesthetic. He had to walk up from his home in the village as he could no longer bicycle. He couldn't drive any more. At first he could barely identify the plants but gradually touch complemented his residual vision. My father's collapse came after Albert had succeeded in re-moulding his life to a new pattern.

My mother in her early fifties was faced with a completely new life. Up to now it had been one of relative ease and comfort. She had made no major decisions. She had depended on William for everything. He was the lynch pin of their lives. Now all was changed. As the months went by it was clear that my father would never recover or work again. My mother's livelihood had to be reviewed.

The business had to be sold and thought given as to where they might live.

In order to make some money and get out of the house some of the time, I got two small jobs doing the accounts of local farmers. Unpredictably I was beginning to feel better in myself. An old friend took me to a couple of dances. I went to a lecture series in Norwich and met John. I would need a full-time job soon. I was twenty eight and desperate to get married and have children. I now knew that a dedicated, celibate life was not for me.

Dr C visited my father weekly. One day he said:

"I think your father has stabilised to some extent. It's now six months since his last stroke. He could have another at any time or he could go on like he is for years."

That night I told my mother I would have to get a job and leave home.

"But you can't...I can't manage Daddy on my own"

"I think we must consider a nursing home for him..."

"Never...I don't want him to have to leave his home, ever."

Mary and family came to stay.

"We think its all become too much for you and Mummy. We think Daddy should go into a home...we'll go and have a look at some while we are here. You need to get away, Ann".

This sounded like a marvellous release. As if I was being given permission to go. But I felt torn with guilt. I wrote to Father Dominic. He answered that I should stay with my parents.

"If you leave your Daddy now, you'll never forgive yourself."

After a week or two I responded to an advert in a farming journal and got a job as 'statistics officer' in an agricultural chemical company just outside Cambridge. I felt jubilant as if a door had been flung open. I also felt extremely guilty. My mother was very upset and wept.

"You're all forcing me to put him into a home and I think it's quite wrong. He should be able to stay here."

The family trustees patiently explained to her that she couldn't remain indefinitely at Langley Hall Farm.

"Can't we buy it?"

"Well no. The Langley estate is all being sold and they want a higher price for the house than we feel you can afford at present."

In April 1955 we moved my father into a local nursing home and I left for Cambridge.

It was a strange spring. I walked on the Backs after work. It was only six years since the pre-Crucible visit with my mother, but it felt much longer. I looked at the primroses and crocuses in the college gardens. I went home some weekends to see my father.

He was making extraordinary efforts to appear 'normal'. He seemed to be responding to the respect he was accorded by the staff. He was much thinner but was dressed in a suit with a tie. He was behaving like a perfect gentleman. When we visited he scarcely noticed us. There was no sign of the 'regressed' behaviour of recent months. This change in him, although welcome, also made me feel very uneasy. What was going on?

My mother was desperately unhappy.

"He shouldn't be there, Ann. He ought to be in his own home.

I visited friends in Lancashire for the August Bank Holiday. My mother phoned:

"Please come home at once. He's had another stroke."

It was a long and complicated train journey because of the holiday. By the time I got to the home he had died and been laid out in their chapel. I was horrified at the changes in him since my last visit. He was a skeleton. He had a considerable beard. What had happened to him? He looked very like the marble effigy of the Tudor Sir William Petre in the chantry chapel of Ingatestone parish church. Was this really my ever acerbic, weighty, round faced dad? He seemed to have been absorbed by his ancestor into an aesthetic, poised and very sad Petre. I wept for the Dads I had lost. The lives we had had and not had.

For me there would always remain the question of how far my joining the Crucible had helped to cause his illness and decline. Back then I wondered what had been achieved by my joining the Crucible. What was wanted of me next?

After the funeral, attended by half Norfolk, I went back to Cambridge. Three months later John and I married. We lived in Cambridge for the next twenty years raising three sons.

Helen's Story

1957 – 1982

and

Mother's Diary 1960

After Helen left boarding school, she trained at Elizabeth Arden in London, to become a beautician. She shared a flat with friends. In 1957, when she was eighteen, she began to keep a scrapbook of the social events in her life.

She had been popular and left school with a wide friendship network. Like many 'only' children, or ones with much older siblings, she found her peer group important to her. She was always careful to keep in touch with her friends; remembering their birthdays and so on. All her life she was sought after. Like her father she was very reserved but she was also good at parties and helping people to enjoy themselves. Some may have felt her laughter was occasionally forced, her contralto voice too deep, others thought they were attractive.

By eighteen Helen had already had severe losses in

her life. At two she had lost her nanny. At eight she went to a boarding prep school. At ten her big sister joined the Crucible. Fairly soon after this her Daddy became ill and started being different. She was doubtless aware of what her mother was suffering. Like many 'last' children, she felt very responsible for the well being of her parents, her family, and ultimately her wider world. Her holidays, from the age of eleven until her father's death when she was sixteen, must have been overshadowed by his terrible illness and insanity. Helen hid her pain.

Little wonder that her scrapbook shows a life of social whirl. On the first page she pasted a programme for 'Share my Lettuce', a musical diversion, at the Comedy Theatre, written by Bamber Gascoine with a first performance on 25th September 1957. Maggie Smith was described as 'in Orange', and Kenneth Williams in 'Lettuce Green'. Helen evidently dined at Casa Pepe in Soho and went to see 'Roar like a Dove' at the Phoenix. These programmes and the rest in the scrapbook, all cost sixpence. She went to 'Salad Days' at the Vaudeville and 'Dear Delinquent' with Anna Massey, David Tomlinson, and Helen's uncle, Aubrey Dexter.

By 1958 Helen had moved to a job in Cambridge as a junior beautician at Joshua Taylor's shop. First she stayed with us in the Avenue but soon moved out to share a flat with friends in Park Parade. Invitations from undergraduates poured in. She went to point-to-points, balls, cocktail parties and even to watch motor racing at Snetterton. There's the dance programme for the Asparagus Club ball at Trinity Hall for March 7th 1958 – Quickstep, Waltz, Latin American, Slow Foxtrot, Quickstep, Waltz Medley, Slow

Foxtrot (Elimination), Eightsome Reel, Asparagus Toast, Cabaret, and then another itemised nine dances. Did she dance them all?

How did she fit in going to work? She had invitations from all over the region including Essex and Norfolk. Her friends started to get married and she went to their weddings. The undergraduate invitations are delightfully formal, on nicely printed cards. On June 6th Nicholas Luard, Jonathan Parker, Adam and Michael Ridley, with William Quiller, were At Home with cocktails at 6.30 pm in The Fellows Garden, Magdalene (if wet in Benson Hall).

What was happening at this time to our mother? She did not leave many records of her life but her diary for 1960 and little notebooks she kept of her visits to America in the sixties and seventies speak a lot of her relationship to Helen.

After William died in 1955 my mother stayed on at Langley Hall Farm until 1959. She was desperately unhappy and during those years thought about where else she might live. She did not want to stay on at Langley and financially it was hardly an option.

She thought she might like to live halfway between Mary and Helen in London and ourselves in Cambridge. She looked at various houses in Hertfordshire but found nothing she liked. Then in January 1959 the house called Dilston in Ingatestone became available. It had been built quite recently for Mary Petre, my father's eldest sister. But she only lived in it a short while before she died. It was a charming contemporary house with a good sized garden and it had been built in a corner of the old Tor Bryan park, next door to the Catholic Church built by my grandfather.

The executors of my father's estate suggested that my mother consider moving into Dilston. She was reluctant at first but realised that the existing connections between the family and the village were in the house's favour.

She moved in July 1959 and faced the fresh bereavement of leaving her married home with all its sad and happy memories. We knew nothing of Grief Counselling in those days. We relied on our friends, our doctor and the church. Perhaps professional help, as is available today, would have helped our mother very much. She was a gallant woman and the 1960 diary represents something of a fresh start for her.

"January 1ˢᵗ. Another year begins. I'm going to be like Mrs Dale. [1]

I wonder how many days I shall miss."

She plainly made tremendous efforts to build herself a new life:

Sunday, January 3rd * Resolution: to be in church by 10.30, can pray and say the rosary. A lovely quiet but busy day. Singing so high I must ring D. about harmonium. Mrs F.J. asks me for coffee on Tuesday. Later the Ingrams invite me for coffee Thursday. Look at garden. Write letters. Listen to radio. Eventually at 5.45 I have a nice tea at the Yorkshire Tea Rooms. What *dear girls they are. Back to clean all the silver and make soup in the pressure cooker." The next day she visits an old lady in a local nursing home and promises to go again in a few days time. The next day "two men arrive to put in more shrubs. They started on the drive and made the rose bed smaller. So sunny and birds singing." A few days later she has "a dreary day as I can't find my key and the coal I ordered never came. I have let the fire out and feel cold and scratchy..."*

During the year she moves about a lot. She goes to London and to Cambridge several times to visit her children and help out with her grandchildren. She goes back to Langley to visit friends there. She goes on a trip with a friend to Scotland and to Rome. She cooks a lot for friends and family and tries out new recipes.

Maybe some of the activity was a defence against the sadness that is 'out there' and hinted at occasionally. She thinks a lot about Helen and is distressed when Helen doesn't ring her before leaving for a holiday in Austria.

"Rang Helen twice. No reply. She might have rung me. The young are selfish. She knows I am alone and how much I long to see her or even hear her. One can always fit in time for one's mother...I don't like to ring her in case she's in bed. So I say some Hail Mary's for her instead."

Helen may have found my mother's affection oppressive at times. It was a difficult situation for both of them. Helen celebrated her 21st Birthday with a party in London to which our mother went. Helen's activities were subsidised by her mother who wished she would give up smoking as she has a nasty bronchial cough.

On August 20th she has some confrontation with Helen over money for clothes. This upsets Marjorie very much:

"Helen isn't kind. She doesn't mean it. I'm so stupid and talk too much...I am a garrulous mama. I am very sad at heart and lonely inside and a pain is always there for darling William's pain...I must turn my pain to benefit not inward ugliness. Take a sleeper. Wake at 6 a.m., make tea and write this."

Helen goes to Italy to try and get a job, possibly as an au pair. On September 10th there's a diary entry:

"Go confession. Fr says 'Go more often to H.Communion for depression!' Shall try an extra mass a week."

During that autumn she has bad headaches and mentions feeling ill and lonely. Helen tries for a job in Rome as she wasn't able to get one in Turin. On October 11th:

"Tragedy...when I get back from mass I'd left birdcage open and one birdie gone!! Leave cage out but no return. Search later. No luck feel so sad, dream about her. I've over watered a plant and all the buds are falling off, misery me...another lovely letter from Helen...head aches and feel weary and low spirited. Darling William would have been 72 today."

Two days later she comes over all queer and i
sick.

On October 17th;

"No 2 budgie flies away!! I had to laugh at my stupid.
but very sad all the same. Glass was a bit loose and s
wriggled out."

But on October 28th she buys, a replacement, 'Litt
Albert'.

On November 11th Helen returns from Italy and
down to Dilston for the weekend. She couldn't get a jo
Rome but is going to try next in Greece.

On November 20th Marjorie goes to Langley and vi
Albert and his family.

"I feel depressed as he's never coming now I realised. I'm
glad he's more content and has put on some weight."

It is clear from this entry that she had held on to t
hope that Albert and his wife Minnie would move and li
in Ingatestone near her. I imagine she became even mo
depressed as that is her last diary entry for 1960.

❖ ⋅⋅⟶⊜ ⊜⟻⋅⋅ ❖

In the early nineteen sixties Helen got a job at Elizabetl
Arden in New York. She went to the US embassy to get hei
visa. There she got chatting to a young man P. who was
planning to go to San Francisco in California. There was
a lot of queuing and waiting so Helen and P. talked for an

hour or more. They agreed to meet up sometime in the US if either got across the continent to visit the other.

We were all sad to see Helen go but we also felt it was a great adventure for her. Our mother must have missed her very much. She started to suffer badly from eczema. As ordinary medication did not seem to be helping she tried homeopathic remedies. By 1963 she was so ill she went in to a London nursing home. There she told me that she felt her skin was weeping for her spirit. Her skin was shedding flakes to such an extent that a dustpan was used, daily, to sweep it up from the floor around her bed. After a few months it seemed as if she had reached rock bottom and, very slowly, she started to heal.

Meanwhile, Helen stayed in New York until she had saved enough to share a car with friends and make a great crossing of the continent to California. On her arrival she wrote to her mother on August 4th, 1965:

"So much has been happening. I shall have to send you a copy of our route as I wrote it all down. San Francisco is wonderful. I have completely fallen in love with it. Much smaller than New York. Lovely houses. Small and bright and so clean. Everyone looks happy and smiling. People are pleased to help. Not the tension and rush of New York."

Helen was to spend the rest of her short life in California. Her delight in its people never wore thin for her.

She started a job at Elizabeth Arden almost straighta-way. Her letter speaks of a social life starting as well. Very

quickly she picked up with friends like P. from the embassy encounter and made new ones.

In May 1966 our mother made her first trip to California. Helen put her up in her apartment and had friends who would entertain her while she, Helen, went to work. Marjorie stayed several weeks and there were times of tension, recorded in the notebook our mother kept. By this time Helen no longer had the rounded figure of a twenty year old. She was to our mother's eyes too thin. Her smoking was still a contentious issue. She ate less than our mother would have liked. Marjorie began to fear she was anorexic. In those days there was much less understanding of why young women, in particular, might have 'eating difficulties.'

"A really wonderful day, so sunny and beautiful. After 8.30 mass Helen goes off to her barbecue with P. and Mrs M and her daughter pick me up. We go to nearly the top of Mount Tamelpais to see a simply wonderful performance of 'Peer Gynt on the Mountain'. We eat picnic lunch sitting on stones in the amphitheatre. Plays have been done here since 1913 with the stone seats built later by out-of-work men."

Helen started going out with P and in February 1967 they were married in a fine Catholic Church on the Broadway. P was not a catholic but Helen remained a very devout one all her life. Marjorie and her sister Mariel Dexter were the only members of Helen's family able to go to the wedding. Mary and I were too busy with small children and we could not afford the air fares. The photos show a radiant Helen in a simple white satin dress. P. was an engineer working with air conditioning firms. They spent the next few years in San Francisco or in Auburn; about one hundred and twenty miles north of S.F. where they eventually bought a plot of land on which they planned to build their own home. They had Marjorie to stay several times.

In 1970 Marjorie stayed with them in S.F. and they drove her up to Meadow Vista, Auburn. Her diary records:

"Long drive. P. goes early to mend water pipe. H and I stop at Coffee House half way. P. cooks a barbecue (meat a bit tough!)."

Once again the diary mentions some tensions and frictions. Helen is even thinner by now but cannot bear her mother remonstrating with her to 'eat more.' They take her on wonderful trips to Lake Tahoe and into Nevada

During 1970 and 1980 Marjorie visited Helen and P. several times and they came to see us over here. Helen was extremely thin but she seemed energetic. We probably only saw her when her illness was in remission. Marjorie was worried about her but always thought she was thin because she didn't eat enough.

Marjorie moved from Dilston to Courts Cottage, outside Haslemere in North Sussex in 1972. There she seemed to live the same kind of life as she had had in Essex. She worked for her local Catholic Church, she had quite a circle of friends, and she enjoyed eating out in Haslemere. She had a charming cottage with a good sized garden and a dog she loved. But happiness and true content eluded her. As she aged she grew lonelier and more depressed, especially in the long, dark winters. She would telephone me in the evenings and say: "Tell me some good news".

---

[1] *Mrs Dale's Diary was a popular radio programme in the sixties.*

144

Hospital School

1974

"One day I overheard two domestics discussing the ward, as they drank a cup of coffee in the canteen sitting-room.

'Where are you working now?'

'Skylark!'

'You know what they call Skylark? Heartbreak Ward!'

'You never finish do you? Feed them…clean up the mess…and it's time to start getting the tea ready'

'Heartbreak Ward!' I sat there thinking. The two young women had expressed the root of the frustration felt by most people who worked on that ward." [1]

There were thirty dependent children and young people and often only three or four nursing staff to cope with all their needs. They worked a thirteen hour day. At the weekends when there was no school or occupational therapy it was a non-stop slog of washing, feeding, changing, clearing up. A sense of the children's unmet needs made staff feel inadequate and frustrated.

The hospital built in the sixties housed 300 patients. These ranged from babies to fifty-year-olds. In those days their IQ's were considered to be in the 0–50 spectrum. Some of the patients had behaviour problems as well as severe learning difficulties. It was thought to be a forward looking hospital. Its main problem seemed to be a lack of funding for sufficient staff.

The hospital had a school but it was not possible to get children there if they were in wheelchairs and their wards were too far away. On these wards 'school' was set up daily in an empty room. My first experience of teaching was in a dayroom on Skylark Ward.

Bringing up my own children was no preparation for life on a sub-normality ward. I had not done a teacher's training. Nothing had warned me about the results of incontinence. I got the position through being a volunteer on the ward, my degree, and the publication of a handbook I had written for parents of children going into general hospitals.[2]

During The 'Swinging Sixties' I had become involved with the movement to liberalise the treatment of children and their parents in hospital. I helped to start the Cambridge group of *Mother Care for Children in Hospital*. In 1967 the organisation, renamed, the *National Association for the Welfare of Children in Hospital*, sent me as their representative to a conference in Philadelphia that launched a parallel US organisation called the *America Association for Children in Hospitals*. I wrote articles about children for a number of magazines and newspapers. I became a governor of Addenbrookes Hospital with a special brief to watch out for the needs of children and their parents.

In 1971, keen to get a salaried job, I went on a part time re-orientation course at the North London Polytechnic. The course sent me as a volunteer to the hospital school. Then I got the chance to join the school staff.

We were employed by the local education authority. My assistant and I visited the school building at the start of each day and at its end. On the ward we felt like being in a remote outpost. The head visited us every day on her bicycle. Not surprisingly some of the ward staff found the idea of trying to educate these children hard to grasp. Mostly they were glad to have us there. If we helped out with changing the children when the ward was very short staffed the distinction between us and them virtually disappeared.

The ward charge nurse, like many in the hospital, was from overseas.

He was an extremely attractive Italian. I found working on the ward was immensely shocking after years cooped up at home. I'd never had much experience of what might be called the real world apart from the recent writing forays. My childhood had been sheltered, then Oxford and then The Crucible, marriage and home. The physical sensations were bewildering. I felt my body erupting. I began to feel –for the first time– highly aroused sexually. It was weird, frightening and exciting. The ward scenario was charged, in the oddest way it was erotic. Maybe it was because of the constant pressure of the physical need, the constant handling of other people's bodies. Probably as a defence against the tragedy that lay around them, ward staff kept up an unremitting barrage of fairly coarse banter. Sexual innuendo waited at every turn.

I 'fancied' the charge nurse, Marco. Many did. He flirted mildly with everyone, but not with 'the teacher'. That would have been unprofessional. He kept me at a respectful arm's length. Plainly he did not reciprocate my feelings for him and, foolishly, I felt rejected.

My assistant Elizabeth and I worked hard every day to transform the dayroom into a stimulating environment for the children. We set out the room like a normal nursery school with areas for sand and water play, painting and 'messy' activities. Each of the seventeen children had a programme with goals suitable for their stage of development. Because each child needed one-to-one help we were glad that the physiotherapists worked alongside us. We had a number of volunteers, professional placements, university students, secondary school children. Whenever it was warm enough we would get the children out of doors.

Occasionally we had a whole ward outing. On a day when we were coming back from Great Yarmouth, Marco, came and sat beside me on the coach.

"You and Elizabeth work very hard. You do more for the children than the last teachers – you do not mind what you do, we like that."

"I think everyone has had a good day out…"

His praise was very acceptable. I liked the man. He did not spare himself and was devoted to the children. His staff appreciated him.

A few days later I was in his office.

"You like religious art, Marco?" I was looking at a framed picture of La Pieta, hung above his desk. He looked a little distressed.

"It's my wife's picture. I brought it in from home...she's away with the children."

"Is she also from Italy?"

"No, from Ireland."

He looked as if he felt he had strayed across our professional boundary. I returned to the classroom. Elizabeth told me that Marco and Maria had had a falling out. They were known to have a tempestuous relationship. She'd walked out before.

The following week was half term. It was only when I stopped the daily routine of going to work, that I realised how drained I felt. Marco was on my mind. What was it like to go home to a hospital flat when it was empty? I felt possessive. Did he have other women in? I lectured myself about being teenage and ridiculous. It happened that on the Saturday morning I went to have coffee with a friend in the village near the hospital. On the way home, on impulse I decided to call on Marco.

He was a while answering the bell. He looked very much the worse for wear – unshaven, unwashed and stinking of cigarettes and drink. His puzzled expression gave way to one of fury.

"You have no right to come round here, Mrs Hales...you

are a good teacher but you have no right to spy on me...
please go home to your husband and family and leave me
in peace." With that he slammed the door.

I felt deeply humiliated.

The Avenue where we had lived since 1958 was a middle
class enclave. A lot of neighbourly entertaining went on.
The children went to each other's birthday parties. Sunday
morning drinks parties were frequent. The neighbours
were curious about my new employment and some of the
obvious effects this was having. I splashed out on 'exciting'
new clothes – long plaid skirts, bright Brutus shirts with
large turn back cuffs and collars in shocking pink, lime
green, turquoise. I used to borrow my teenage sons' flares.
At local gatherings I was aware of slightly more male attention. Some of the women were a touch critical.

"You won't be able to keep up the coffee morning rota?
What a shame"

"What will you do about the school run?"

"A second salary must make such a difference. I suppose
you'll have a holiday abroad this summer?"

"We think it's quite marvellous of you"

"Glad to see you emerging from your chrysalis. I knew
you would one day"

We were invited to a lot of parties that Christmas including a New Year's Eve dance near Thetford. I had known
Richard, our host, since childhood. I had had a teenage
crush on him. He was several years older than me and I

had always carried a tiny flag for him. In 1943 he was called up and I went to Oxford. By the time I was back in Norfolk in 1954 he had married Clare, a talented ceramicist, and they lived between Norwich and Cambridge. During my father's last illness I used to go over to spend time with them. By now he had qualified as an archaeologist. After I married we kept in touch and they usually invited us to their New Year's Eve party.

I knew I looked good that evening. I had a white satin dress and since working at the hospital I had lost weight and gained confidence. During the course of the evening I felt Richard was seeking me out. We danced several times.

"It's amazing Ann, how you've changed. It's great the work you are doing. I find hospitals of any kind difficult to cope with". I warmed to his admiration and was delighted when he murmured:

"I want to see more of you than at these annual parties. I have to come to meetings in Cambridge. Can I ring you at the hospital?" From his Greek mother Richard had inherited an olive skin, brown eyes and thick curling dark hair. He was very physical, moving with grace and co-ordination. He'd always had great charm and was fun to be with. He teased me like my Grandpa used to when I was getting over-serious.

At the hospital work finished for me most Fridays at noon. Richard and I met for lunch several times.

Our affair began against a background of hospital life. For me the excitement of our meetings was intensified by the suffering of the children. The poignancy of their spirits imprisoned in their impaired bodies, was with me all the time in those days. In my dreams I was always pushing heavy wheel chairs.

Brief meetings with Richard were a wonderful escape from the hard work of a job and home life. Although it wasn't true I felt I had waited for Richard a long time, since I was about fourteen. In an unreal way he had always belonged to me. It seemed like a miracle to be so wanted at forty eight.

Back at home with teenagers pouring into the house and loud music pouring out of it I envied what my sons seemed to have – youth, good looks and the world opening out. By the seventies the strict moral imperatives that had ruled my life until then, had begun to weaken.

After our first love-making I was convinced that this was what I had always waited for.

---

[1] *The Children of Skylark Ward, Teaching Severely Handicapped Children, Cambridge University Press, 1978, p.93*

[2] *Children in Hospital: the Parents' View, Priory Press, 1973.*

Journey into Solitude

Erat Hora

1975

"Erat Hora"

One hour was sunlit...

Ezra Pound [1]

She lay on her back looking up at the ash trees that were still bare of leaves. At first the sun shone above his head, but as the day wore on, it shone over his left shoulder. That was how she would always remember the spring and summer – his head illumined from behind by the dazzling pale gold sun. He was a god from the Mediterranean.

She had been afraid to give herself to him. Ashamed of her body. He did not hurry her. She explained her feelings, her diffidence. He said very little. His hand held hers and as she talked the sun shone through patterned branches. A cuckoo encircled the wood with its persistent echolalic call. First close, then far away, making a ring of magic that shielded the wood from time. A robin flew close to observe them, and sang to claim his patch of the woods. Pigeons sustained a reassuring lullaby. Gradually her fears subsided. Some way off, between the trees, a herd of deer slipped by, the sun catching their antlers as they moved, silently, from light to shadow.

She turned to him. His response was tender and urgent. From then on she was his, whatever came.

All she had ever felt about woods came together that day. In the early evening she found a branch that had fallen and lodged against another tree. She walked along it several feet above the ground and looked out over a green sea of dogs mercury, ruffled into waves by the breeze, just as in the bluebell wood at home. She listened to the silence as she used to listen in her Norfolk wood. At last a circle was complete. Now she was grasping something that had painfully eluded her as a six year old. The sensation that something infinitely precious was just out of reach, was gone. What she had always thought was a yearning for Infinite Beauty was now satisfied. This man, she now knew, was the missing part of her.

The cuckoo's call that" caps, clears and clinches all" was woven through an April day that would define her life…

Things might have turned out very differently if she had not chosen to ignore the little inner warning that the cuckoo is one of Nature's successful deceivers.

❧⸺⊙⸺❦

Then it was Holy Week. She was staying in a garden suburb. It was Palm Sunday. She could not miss Mass and Communion. Suddenly she realised she was trapped. She loved God and she wanted to follow the rituals of Holy Week, she wanted to share in Christ's passion and resurrection, but she had committed adultery. It was a brutal word for a happening that filled her with a sacramental joy and a sense of oneness with God and the universe.

She knew she had to go to confession, and yet she felt it was not a great sin she had to confess. She reconciled herself, for the time being, to inconsistency.

She went to look for a Catholic church. Eventually she found a chapel in a quiet cul-de-sac. There was to be a Mass but no sign that confessions were being heard. She approached the plump, strict-looking priest.

"It's not convenient to hear confessions just before Mass. I always get this happening. I'm single-handed, you know; you really ought to come at the proper times, they're all up on the notice board..."

Her courage faltered.

"Oh! Well, Father, it's not convenient I'll come another day."

He looked at her for the first time. His conscience troubled him. Perhaps he'd been too brusque...he'd had a wretched night with indigestion. She had a desperate look about her. Perhaps if he did not hear her confession she would not come back before Easter.

"All right, but you'll have to be quick. I've got to vest for Mass, you know. Don't make a habit of this."

Gratefully she breathed her thanks.

In the dark, stuffy confessional she listened to her own voice:

"Forgive me Father, for I have sinned. I have committed adultery. For this and all the other sins I cannot remember, please give me absolution."

"Well, my child, this is Holy Week, time for a fresh start. Tell God you are sorry for your sins, unite your sufferings to those of Christ on the cross, and for your penance make the Stations of the Cross, and now I will give you absolution."

Soothingly the words flowed…

"And I in God's name forgive you. Go now and sin no more…Please remember me in your prayers."

Out of the confessional he bustled down the church. A man, who had waited to have his confession heard, was dismissed with a wave.

"Not now. I'm already late. I'm single-handed you know, confession times are on the board."

Weak-kneed she crept into the nearest pew. Later as she approached the altar to receive communion she felt she was watching someone out of a Graham Greene novel. What did 'a firm purpose of amendment', and 'avoiding the dangerous occasions of sin' mean now?

"Lord, what am I to do?"

She listened. Silence. No harsh condemnation. Just stillness. Tears trickled down her face.

"Lord, I cannot see."

"The Mass is ended. Go in peace to love and serve the Lord."

She remained kneeling. Gradually the tears dried. Slowly the church emptied.

She walked down the aisle and out into a perfect spring morning.

Large houses gleamed in their trim gardens. Daffodils and red polyanthus edged freshly mown lawns. Almond blossom scattered on grass verges in a light breeze. Husbands were leathering immaculate Rovers and Volvos. A milk van trundled by. At the bottom of the hill it stopped to do deliveries. She bought a pint of milk knowing she had missed breakfast at the college, where part of her, it seemed, was at a hospital conference. She returned to a day of agendas, resolutions, speeches. But as she sat there, half listening, she was suffused with new warmth. She hugged her new secret to herself. 'I am special...I am loved...I am lovable, desirable'.

But she also knew that what had happened to her lately had long knock on consequences.

"No man is an island…never send to know for whom the bell tolls…"

---

[1] *Selected Poems by Ezra Pound, Faber, 1948*

Love's Limbeck

1975

"Study me then, you would lovers be
At the next world that is, at the next spring
For I am every dead thing,
In whom love wrought new alchemy...
I, by love's Limbeck, am the grave
Of all that's nothing..."

John Donne

At Oxford a friend had said:

"I worry about you, Ann. You are so impulsive. One day, I'm afraid, you'll do something really stupid that will land you in serious trouble."

Nowadays she might have used the epithet 'self-destructive'. This friend went on to become an ambassador.

It was a midsummer of sweltering heat. Wheat shimmered. Willows twisted nervous leaves. Poppies and purple vetch caught at their legs, trailing brambles scratched them. Their bodies melted in the midday glare. Limbs glistened with sweat. In a hollow, under white hawthorn, they talked. She had waited ages for him and had been beginning to despair. Then across the fields, she saw him coming. The moment of meeting. The dreary, long wait over.

She felt she would crush the life out of him. All the hoping since they last met, weeks ago. The not knowing when they would meet again.

Once she waited for him all day and walked through a wood in blinding panic. What had happened? Had someone found out? Had he had an accident? Is this how it would end? The thought of judgment was strong. Was this the punishment? She heard the distant slam of a car door. She felt dizzy, suffocated. He came towards her, arms outstretched, face pale and taut:

"It was God! It was God!"

In fact, it had been a fractured exhaust pipe miles from anywhere. He was tired and tense. The bright day was ruined. It began to grow cloudy. A sharp breeze sprang up. The wood stirred uneasily. They made love but achieved nothing. As they left the wood she saw the bluebells had run to seed.

Summer turned to autumn. Weeks lengthened into months. Had he ended with her? She hated the way she was dependent on him. She had let him take over her life. It was chaotic and disordered. She had no peace of mind.

One stormy day in November he rang her on the ward.

"Meet me in the Carpenters Arms, tomorrow, lunchtime. I'll explain everything."

The pub was near the hospital. They sat by a fire. It was pouring with rain.

"I've been on a dig in Yorkshire…I've missed you…Where can we meet in this weather?"

"I wish you'd been in touch…Didn't know what was going on…It's been so long…"

His face shut down.

"Don't go on please. I've had a bellyful of that at home… that's partly why I went on this dig. It's a very interesting complex of…"

"Has she *guessed?* Does she know?"

"I'm not sure…she's pretty intuitive about these things…"

"It's happened before you mean?"

"Ann, we're all grown ups here…where do you suggest we meet and have a proper talk."

"Well I have a friend in this village. She's away a lot…she might let me have her garden hut, no questions asked."

"Has it got heating? I can't bear being cold…"

"I could probably organise a stove."

❖⬩⟩━◉ ◉━⟨⬩❖

The hut was warm. The stove which smelled of paraffin shed a circle of light on the wooden roof. Candles made it a stable, glowing like a Rembrandt. It was warm inside the sleeping bag on a pile of cushions. He slid his long body in beside hers.

For once they were happy and relaxed. The usual pre-occupations with families and future, guilt and regret, were put aside.

Looking at his beautiful face in total repose, after making love, she marvelled. She breathed a thank you prayer for all that had come to her at this stage of her life. Lately, with all the pain and anxiety, she felt she had joined the human race, at last. 'My beloved came to me, and I was glad.' She was very influenced by her reading of Iris Murdoch.

"Intense erotic love, love which involves with the flesh all the most refined sexual being of the spirit, which reveals and perhaps even ex nihilo creates spirit as sex, is comparatively rare in this inconvenient world." [1]

It is doubtful whether he saw their meetings in a garden hut in such literary terms. Ann read on and made notes...

"This love presents itself as such a dizzily lofty value that even to speak of 'enjoying' it seems a sacrilege. It is something to be undergone upon one's knees. And where it exists it cannot but shed a blazing light of justification upon its own scene, a light which can leave the rest of the world dark indeed." [2]

The friend had gone abroad for the winter. They met in her hut a number of times. He explained his mood swings. He felt he had a cycle of six weeks going down when he got more and more depressed and withdrawn. Then he would begin to feel more energetic and optimistic. This phase would last several weeks before he started going down again. An emotional upset, a financial or family crisis might precipitate the downward slide,

She felt that the gentle, empathic man in his 'hopeful' weeks was a world away from the depressed Richard. She now realised that the unpredictable pattern of their meetings was partly related to these variations in his mood.

One day she was sitting in their local with her husband when Clare and Richard came in. She usually spoke first.

"We thought we'd come slumming," she laughed. "We've both had meetings in Cambridge this morning". She sat down. Richard went for drinks.

"We're so excited, we're off to Brittany next week…we'll be house hunting!"

"Are you moving?"

Richard was in a withdrawn mood. His eyes looked cold.

"Well it hasn't got as far as that, not by a long chalk."

"Why Brittany?"

"I've got a cousin who wants us to buy a house with her, and I could have a much larger kiln and they like my work over there".

"What will you do, Richard?"

Clare burst in again:

"That's the great thing…we'll look in Vannes which is near all those incredible prehistoric sites that Richard has always wanted to work on…Haven't you, my darling?"

"I'll have to get a job first."

"Let's drink to Brittany!"

It was the Easter holidays. They were off to North Norfolk in a week's time. Would she see him before she left? It was typical April weather, sunshine and showers. Their kitchen calendar had this quote under the picture of a graveyard with daffodils:

> *"O, how this spring of love resembleth*
> *The uncertain glory of an April day,*
> *Which now shows all the beauty of the sun,*
> *And by and by a cloud takes all away."*

(Two Gentlemen of Verona)

The days ticked by. How could she face going away without even a word from him? "I've got to get used to this" she said to herself. "If they go to France, I may not see him for years. They might even be gone by the time we are back." She did all the necessary things you do before taking a family away. She felt disembodied as if her spirit was floating six inches above her head. It was someone else who made lists, bought groceries, sorted books, games, clothes, and packed.

The day before they left she saw him in the market square. He came over and kissed her tenderly on the mouth.

"See you when you're back. Enjoy our windswept coast!" With a wave he was gone.

So that was it. Was it enough? It had to be.

It was extremely cold that week in North Norfolk. The cottage had very little heating. They went for long bracing walks on Holkham beach and took the boat from Blakeney to see the seals. She and her husband were civil to each other, but she knew there was an unhappy atmosphere. She hated herself for causing this. Until now they had had such wonderful family holidays, and she did love them all so much.

The summer term began. The children were taller and she was thinner than a year ago, and smoking.

A week went by, two, three. One day she was at the station meeting a friend and Richard came past in the crowd coming off the King's Cross train. She looked at him and smiled. He looked shamefaced and truculent.

"Will I see you soon?"

"Yes, soon." He managed a half smile. That was all she got.

She knew she was obsessed with him. It felt like an addiction. One glimpse of him in a crowd had left her feeling weak, disoriented.

A week later. For once he was there in the wood before her. As she came through the trees she saw him stretched out on the grass in characteristic pose, arms behind his head, relaxed, nonchalant. Like James in the Margaret Drabble novel she was reading. Passion washed over her, he was so stylish, so beautiful, and so Grecian. She ran towards him and fell into his arms.

"Oh! My beautiful one...I do love you."

He undid her blouse. He'd never said that before, and he never said it again.

Later he told her that France was off. He was going back to the dig in Yorkshire.

"Too hot at home?"

"Something like that."

A few days later she was making bread. There was a pounding on the door. It was a distraught Clare

"I've been setting up a pottery show in King's Parade and the department has just phoned to say that Richard has fallen in Yorkshire and broken several bones. They're taking him by ambulance to the Norfolk and Norwich. I'm off there now."

"Oh! Clare, what can I do?"

"I thought you ought to know..."

"Shall I tell anyone for you?"

But she'd rushed off.

He had complicated fractures of his left arm and leg. She visited him in hospital and in the distance saw Clare arriving as she I was leaving. The next time she went he said:

"I don't think Clare likes you coming here…I think it would be better if you didn't visit."

"I need support too you know!"

"Yes, but she's my wife and she's been through the hell of a lot…I don't want fuss."

So she didn't visit him at the hospital again.

For a while after his accident their relationship changed. It was less driven. She was made welcome in their house. Sometimes she talked to him on his own. He said he felt he couldn't leave Clare and his children. He urged her to try and make a go of her marriage.

It was mid-July. She'd had a very busy week in school winding things up. In the autumn she was going to a teacher training college to study for a postgraduate certificate in education. One afternoon going home from the hospital she saw his car in the pub yard. He stood on the pavement.

"I'm afraid this is it Ann."

"So you'll just up sticks and end it?"

He looked pale, evasive.

"Well it's had some great moments, but…"

"No Buts, Richard, Please!" She was frightened and angry.

Now he looked angry.

"Well what do you suggest? We can't meet for ever in a garden hut…"

He glanced in her car at all her school paraphernalia.

"Make the best of things. You've got college ahead; pastures new...like the cat you've got nine lives'. This was one of his clichés that she hated.

"I can't stay with him any more, that's not an option... If I leave him and get a place of my own will you come and see me?"

He sighed.

"I'm not making any promises...that's never been our way..."

That night she had a terrible nightmare.

"She couldn't see. It was all dark. She had a man on top of her.

'Is it you, Richard?' But she knew it was her husband trying to force an entry."

The next morning her husband said:

"I was terrified last night. You sang in your sleep...it was high-pitched, eerie, an Ophelia song...it went on for about twenty minutes...I didn't dare wake you up..."

In the end she decided to go to Cornwall on her own for a few weeks. The family went elsewhere for the holidays. Before she left she found a tiny, empty cottage in a fen village. A friendly solicitor did the conveyance in a fortnight.

The next day she left the house and the Avenue, knowing she would never return. She planned to write to her husband from Cornwall. She was afraid to tell him to his face that she was leaving him. Things were so bad between them that she feared he might become violent.

---

[1] *The Sacred and Profane Love Machine by Iris Murdoch, the Viking Press, 1974*

[2] *Ibid. Page 261*

Cornwall

1976

She got a lift to Cornwall in Tony's lorry. He was a porter and driver at the hospital. He also ran a small transport business in his own time. He was a giant, six foot six and very broad. He had rough manners but an educated voice. He also had a disarming grin with only one top tooth. It was alleged that he'd lost the rest in a boxing match. He had a reputation, in the hospital, for drinking and womanising. However he had a clean driving licence and intended keeping it that way.

He was always ready to help with lifting and carrying. He was very gentle with the children who liked him. He drove the hospital coach on ward outings. On one of these she told him she needed to move some furniture from Cambridge to her cottage. When he did this he asked her if she'd like a lift to Penzance as he had to make a run down there with a delivery. He refused any payment.

"Why are you so good to me?" she asked him.

A blush made his large face glow.

"You remind me of the only decent teacher I had. She taught me to read." That was all she got out of him.

173

At four am on a fine August morning he picked her up in Cambridge with her camping gear. She had a huge lump in her throat as they drove down the silent road, away from her home, and past the houses of many friends.

Tony offered her some spearmint. They drove in silence apart from the Beatles singing 'It's a hard day's night' all the way to Royston.

Out of Cambridgeshire, into Hertfordshire and then Middlesex. "What am I doing" she asked herself, "leaving all that is familiar and well loved for a most uncertain future? Am I completely crazy?"

Perched high in the lorry heading steadily south westwards she shifted from being at the heart of a busy family life to being a solitary individual. At that moment she had no ties to any person or place. She felt scared.

During their first stop, eating a large fried breakfast, Tony looked at her and said:

"When I'm driving I concentrate on the road ahead… the next town…what's coming…who's trying to overtake…I don't think about where I've come from…the towns behind me…I reckon you need to do the same…"

It was his longest utterance so far. She mulled it over until their next stop near Chippenham. Here he said:

"I've done what you're doing. Left my wife and kids five years ago. She was messing about with another driver…he'd been one of my best mates…I couldn't stand it…"

"How's it now, Tony?"

"Not easy…I miss them every day, but I don't think I could have done anything different…that's the road behind…"

Later, after they had crossed the Tamar and were in Cornwall, he said:

"I've got another delivery down here in a month's time and could take you back."

This offer felt immensely friendly. It gave an end point to her first bit of self-imposed exile. So much easier to go back with Tony rather than on a coach or train. Above the plangent notes of Abba's 'Dancing Queen', she smiled her relief and acceptance. Echoing her thoughts he said:

"You'll be surprised who comes along…what comes along when you're travelling…and lady are you travelling!"

She laughed.

"Well, Tony, Cambridge to Penzance in eight hours is a good start."

Early in the afternoon they reached Nancledra. It was near this village that she was going to camp. Justin, a volunteer at the hospital, a university student, was down here with a group of friends, for the summer vac. They were demolishing a cottage for a relation of his. He'd said she could camp in the overgrown cottage garden. Justin's directions said to turn right into Burnt Lane opposite the village stores. Soon Tony was forcing the lorry through a green tunnel. On their left a stream tumbled over rocks under ancient trees dripping with lichen and moss. Slowly the lorry pushed on through overhanging boughs. Half a mile from the village they reached a stone bridge on their left. Tony stopped the engine and got out.

"I daren't take her over that."

"No, that's alright. Tony. It's getting late for your delivery anyway. I'll wait here for Justin."

"I can't turn here", he examined her ordinance survey map, "I'll drive on to the next lane junction where I think I can get back to the main road."

He looked anxious.

"You be alright?"

She nodded and gave him a hug.

"I'll be fine…Now get going, and I'll see you outside the village stores in four weeks."

He climbed back into the cab, started the engine, gave a big wave and edged the lorry slowly forwards. At a corner of the lane he disappeared. The silence was startling. Now she heard the stream and the call of birds. She was overcome by a wave of exhaustion and loneliness. She missed Tony. He had piled her gear by the roadside. She sat on the bridge and cooled her feet in the water. Great clumps of monbretia and king cups lined the banks. The sun was very hot. She stretched out on the grass and fell asleep.

"I'm on a train journey with others in the Crucible. There's a twenty minute break between trains and I go to wash some of my clothes. It takes time to do this

and to get them into a bag, still dripping wet. I need to get something to eat as it's going to be a long journey and I'm already hungry. I hurry down to a kiosk with only two minutes to go before the train leaves. There's a queue of two people. I decide to get some crisps and a blackcurrant drink but I've only got a £10 note. I cannot wait. I hurry to the platform. The train is crowded and full of smoke. I am aware that the head of the Crucible is giving me a ticking off for being so late. 'What made you so late?' I tell her. 'That's ridiculous.'

She wakes as a shadow falls across her face. It's Justin.

"Welcome to Nancledra! I'm on my way to the cottage with the pick up so we can take your gear. Jump in!"

✦⸱⸱➡◉➡⸱⸱✦

She started to write using an old Remington balanced on a plank, supported by two rocks, under a stooping apple tree.

"Page 1

Above Nancledra

Nancledra is a village in the district of West Penwith, not far from Land's End. The name Nancledra means, in the ancient Celtic language, The Valley of Sheltered Habitation. Remote in the fields, above this village, one summer, a woman of fifty, sat in a deserted cottage garden, trying to piece together the years that had brought her to that place. A few weeks would give her a time of sheltered habitation. Would she, when it was time to go, face the

second part of her life with a little more understanding
of what it means to be a middle-aged person living in the
last quarter of the twentieth century?"

Having left her husband she felt concerned about him. She was mistaken, as it turned out, to think in dramatic terms. He neither raised a hue and cry, nor pursued her, or took violent action of any kind. She had left him a letter telling him that she was leaving him, and had bought a cottage in Hanchett in the fens. A few days after she got to Nancledra there was a letter from him poste restante in the village post office. He said he was hurt and angry and disappointed in her, but he was not going to jump off a bridge into the Cam. He said neighbours had been very kind and rallied round. He said he would discuss the children when she returned. In a P.S. he wrote:

"I hear Clare and Richard are likely to leave Norfolk. They are apparently house hunting in Yorkshire."

She read his letter, bought some provisions and started to walk back to the cottage. She sat on the stone bridge, again, with her feet in the stream. The damp, luxuriant vegetation smelt of liquorice. Suddenly she caught a memory of building dams in the stream at Tor Bryan. She knew she had been shocked by the P.S. to his letter. In the unreal state in which she had left Cambridge, she had obviously clung to the hope that Richard would not leave the area after all. Now it seemed that he was definitely on the move.

She had not left John for Richard. But she had clung to the hope that she would see Richard fairly often. The question for her, now, was 'can you live on your own without seeing Richard?' She reasoned with herself. 'I have left my marriage because it has become unbearable. I cannot stay in it. I have burst out of the constrictions of a life shaped by the fifties. John and I have been unable to re-negotiate the terms of our marriage. I cannot go back to being the person he married.' She felt she had become enslaved to a life of cooking, cleaning, servicing the needs of four men, as well as, recently, going out to a hard day job, She had allowed this to happen and she couldn't bear it any more.

She returned to the Remington.

"Her life like this landscape is layered. The broken and desolate hills suddenly come into focus, like a picture puzzle whose hidden features have been staring you in the face all the time. What looks like any old pile of boulders suddenly becomes part of an enclosing wall that curves round the side of a hill, with another wall above it, and another wall above that."

Yesterday had been very frightening. She had set out to explore the Iron Age fort called Chun castle. Justin had given her lift to where a path started up across the moors. She had decided to do a painting of Chun Quoit.

"Neolithic people were immensely concerned with death and the sprit's passage to an after life. The colossal megalithic tombs, or quoits, in West Penwith are witness to this reverence. They were built on higher ground often within sight of the sea and faced either the rising or the setting sun. Today they are the remains of much larger

barrows that lay behind the massive stone entrance chambers."

It was a blazing afternoon as she made her way through bracken and whin bushes that scratched her bare legs. As she clambered over a broken wall of the castle, on her way west, towards the quoit, she heard dogs baying. Last night Justin had talked about hunting dogs seen in this area. They were escapees from farms and were living wild. On another wall of the castle, a few hundred yards away, she saw five rough looking sheepdogs silhouetted against the sky. She had seen no one on her walk. The dogs' barking echoed in the stillness. The next moment they had vanished. 'Were they now, or from an earlier time?'

She walked on towards the quoit. It looked like a giant mushroom made of granite. Its capstone seemed moulded over the enormous upright stones. The blue grey stone glittered as the sun caught pockets of quartz.

She collapsed on the turf and started to paint. The stone shapes filled her page. She was fascinated by the illusion that the capping stone rested so gently on the upright boulders that it might have been floating above them. She rubbed her eyes. Suddenly she heard furious barking behind her. A terrified hare raced past the quoit pursued by a pack of dogs. The hare twisted and turned through the heather. The dogs were nearly on it when a second hare shot in the air and made off in another direction. This made the dogs slacken their pace and then divide. As she watched they all disappeared over the wall of the fort.

She was aware of her heart beating very fast. She breathed

a quick prayer. She had to do a bit more to her painting. She worked very fast as the shadows moved across the stones and the sun started to drop in the sky.

About five she packed up her things and examined the ordinance survey. Justin had said he would pick her up near a farm. She found the path and after about half a mile it started to drop down towards a shallow valley. She left the moor land and came into a rough field. Now the farm buildings were in sight. She was looking forward to some human contact. At that moment she saw she was being watched intently by a very large brown bull, standing between her and the gate into the farmyard.

'My God!'

Suddenly she heard the dogs barking. Next minute they tore in a line across the field. The bull immediately moved off in pursuit and she was able to run to the gate.

As she lay in her sleeping bag that night she remembered how frightened she had been and yet also taken care of. Was this some kind of omen for the future?

She dreamt:

"I'm looking across an ocean by the black Cliffs of Fall. At the foot of the cliff is a narrow rocky beach. On this lie four sleeping bodies, wrapped in sackcloth – with just their heads and hands visible. Each corpse, in turn, wakes the others with a loud cry. Then they all stir together, turn over and settle to sleep again, until one wakes them with a terrible cry."

The nightmare woke her up. It was still dark and cold. That cry of primeval pain echoing against the cliffs rang in her head. It was like a Munch painting. 'What have I done to the people who matter most to me?'

As the sky began to lighten she fell asleep again.

This time she dreamt:

"I buy a small pack of gelignite. I put a small bit on a number of bicycles by a signal box on a railway line. The instructions say it will not work for two days. I think about the devastation it will cause when it explodes – perhaps there will be people in the signal box, perhaps a train will be passing and I will feel responsible for all those deaths…No, I must get the stuff off the bikes…I am aware of a gathering sense of urgency…"

Next morning, early, she rang the children from the village call box, to make sure they were alright.

It was the long hot summer of 1976. She had a routine of swimming in a nearby lake before breakfast and then doing several hours on the Remington under the shady apple tree. She felt as if time was in abeyance. She went to a local farm to fetch water and to the village for provisions. Sometimes she painted. In the evening Justin and his friends would come over from the barn. They'd light a fire and sit round drinking. Sometimes they talked of the Cornish legends. One night Justin told them the cuckoo legend about Towedenack Church which was just up the lane.

That night she dreamt:

"Richard is with me in the churchyard.' Please help me to keep the cuckoo in', I beg. I take his hand and a group of family come up the lane and through the lychgate – John, Mary, the children.' Hold hands, hold hands, make a circle round the bush…we have to stop the cuckoo flying away. Then the summer will last for ever.' We run faster and faster round what is now a mulberry bush. Suddenly there's a flapping and a squawking and an enormous bird bursts out of the foliage and flies away over the squat grey tower of Towedenack Church. I sob it's gone, it's gone…"

She wakes sobbing with a terrible sense of loss. 'It's gone, it's gone', but what's gone? What was so precious? Her former life? This summer?

She's aware of a reluctance to leave her peaceful routine and to re-engage with life. She dreads picking up the threads of life back in Cambridgeshire. What will it be like to live in an unknown village, to go to college?

By this time she's wide awake and restless. She pulls on some clothes by the light of the full moon. The garden is full of whispers and shadows. She takes the track towards the lake, past the old engine house and tall chimney of Giew Mine. The track winds up towards the open moor. She hears voices. Further up the track a group of people are walking towards her. Men in rough clothes carrying picks and lanterns, laughing and singing. She crouches deep into the fuchsia hedge. They're tin miners of a century ago, real and yet insubstantial, on their way to work. Their humour and companionship are palpable. They walk on in the direction of the mine.

A few moments later in the stillness she looks at the moon's reflection in the lake. How privileged she is, how cushioned against poverty, disease, discomfort. She remembers what Tony said on the way down:

"You'll never know what lies round the next bend."

A few days later she left Nancledra, the Valley of Sheltered Habitation.

Hanchett

1976

Number 1, Smith's Row, Hanchett had been built from red brick with a pantiled roof, by a Victorian landowner. There were six cottages in the row used, in earlier times, as tied cottages for the farm workers on the estate. Her cottage had not been modernised but it was functional. At the other end of the row was the old forge, originally used for shoeing horses. The present owner did agricultural machinery repairs and made wrought iron gates for garden centres.

The cottage had a good feeling. It was a two up, two down. A bathroom, of sorts, had been made by the last owner in a shed across the backyard. It was unheated and very cold. The cottage had electricity but not gas. The main source of heat was a wood burning stove in the front room. The kitchen faced north over the small garden.

She loved the cottage and it was hers. She had some furniture from her Norfolk home – two tables, four chairs, a bookcase, a desk and a dressing table. She also had two camp beds and some pots and pans.

The cottage opened straight onto the village pavement, but across the road was a green with period cottages on the far side. Very little traffic used the lane. An ancient waterway called a lode linked the village to the river Cam. There was a mediaeval Merchant's house whose owners had imposed taxes, in earlier times, on goods being transported up river from King's Lynn to Cambridge. Shipping goods through the fens had gone on since Roman times. The village had been built where the fens met a chalky upland, making it an edge-of-fen village.

The village had a mixed population. There were some large farms as well as smaller fen holdings. Some families had lived there for centuries and there were newcomers. With house prices in Cambridge rising in the seventies, professional people began moving out into the villages. She was to find the village friendly to newcomers.

As she put her key in the door, on a warm September day, the telephone was ringing.

"Welcome back! Can I come over? I'm in the area tying up loose ends."

She was startled and annoyed. How had he got her number? Was she one of his 'loose ends'? She didn't want anyone there at this moment.

"Are you there?"

"Yes, well…o.k.…how soon?"

"I'm in the back lane…"

The calm she had built up in Cornwall evaporated. She was back with the old turmoil, the uncertainties, and the longings. She left the front door open and busied herself in the kitchen looking for the coffee, she heard his joyful shout:

"It's marvellous…and all yours?"

Their initial hug lacked something of its customary warmth.

"Coffee? Black…no milk yet"

"I'd rather have a glass of wine, toast the new cottage… your new life."

He looked round the small room with its stack of boxes.

"Got the sleeping bag?"

She felt a surge of anger.

"Yes…well…I've been thinking in Cornwall…"

She got no further as suddenly the light from the front window was dimmed by a lorry. Someone knocked.

"Tony!"

"I was passing so I just stopped to see how you were settling in."

"Good to see you, Tony. This seems to be my morning for visitors. Tony this is Richard. This is Tony who helped move my furniture."

"I must be on my way," said Richard, "I'll be in touch" and with that he left.

Tony had a mug of coffee and then started to help her shift the boxes. After an hour the cottage looked much more habitable.

"I must go now!"

"Tony, thank you so much, you've been good to me."

He gave her a huge hug.

"That's it then...?" a tear was moving down his cheek.

She felt like crying too. "I'm afraid so..." How she hated hurting him. Huge, shaggy, toothless, now he looked bereft.

"Well, I'll be on my way...got to get a load to Manchester..."

She stood in her new doorway and watched him drive away.

It was to be several years before she next saw Tony. He was unloading vegetables in the Cambridge market.

"Hi! Tony" He looked at her across a crate of cauliflowers.

"How ye doing, missus? Still in Hanchett?"

"No, I'm back in Cambridge. Tony, I was so sorry last time we met..."

"Don't say anything. Didn't I once say you never knew what lay ahead? I'm glad to have been in one of your adventures. Now I'm in someone else's. Why don't you have a cauliflower?"

She looked down at its creamy firm centre, its ruff of bright green leaves.

"Thanks, Tony".

She never saw him again.

College

1976 – 1977

A few days later Richard was back.

"So how was Cornwall? You're looking very well."

Before she could answer he went on.

"I'm not sure whether it's going to work out for us in Yorkshire."

Something in her chest lurched.

"Oh!"

"I don't like the job. The chap I'm working for is a right sod."

"Clare? How's she?"

"In her element, loves it up there, made a lot of new friends...I'm not sure if I can stick it."

"So what will you do?"

"I don't know yet. I'm looking up one or two local contacts. Seeing how the land lies...there's a lot of interesting work going on in the Peterborough area and I like the bloke in charge".

"So you might come south again?" She tried, unsuccessfully, to keep her tone neutral.

"I'm not sure about anything...I might keep a base in Yorkshire and commute to work..."

"All this sounds very different to how it was before I went to Cornwall. Is there now some future for us?"

She tried not to sound hopeful. He leant forward, refilled their glasses and lit another cigarette.

"Have you got an ashtray?" He was avoiding looking at her.

"Richard!"

"Well," he shrugged," it's one step up from a garden shed – apart from your freezing bathroom – but it's not quite my scene is it?"

"Come here!" He stabbed out his cigarette and held out his arms.

She felt a great rush of desire but she held back.

"I'm not sure that I want..." His mood changed at once.

"For God's sake woman, what *do* you want, make your mind up?"

"Is that the time? I must be off I promised Pamela Hanchett I'd call in, if I was this way"

"You know her?" She was the local landowner.

"I was in the navy with Gerry. Tragic. He had a massive coronary.

They were a great couple; we had a lot of fun there. It's a lovely house. You should get to know her as you live practically at her lodge gates."

He drained his glass and moved towards the door.

"When shall I see you next?" With his back to her he replied:

"Soon, very soon." Reaching the door he turned.

"Despite what it looks like sometimes, I need you very much. You're a good person. Much too good for me. I'll be back". He went out of the door. From the pavement he smiled and blew a kiss. Her hurt and anger drained away. Moments later she heard his car accelerate down the back lane in the direction of the hall.

On the surface life began to settle into a new routine. Carpeted, furnished and warmed by local logs the cottage became something of a nest. Family and friends enjoyed coming to visit.

During the autumn of 1976 she was energised by the excitement of going back to learning. She was the oldest student on her course and was indulged by her peers. They liked coming out to the cottage and there were cheerful parties at the weekends. The college teaching was very good and she found a particular delight in the art department. When it came to the dreaded teaching practice her newly found art skills were put to good use. She enjoyed her spell in a village primary school and the children did well on a project about wild birds.

It all got a lot harder with the second teaching practice this was in a top class of a much larger primary school. She really struggled with teaching maths. She found classroom management and control very difficult. Nothing in the hospital had prepared her for teaching a class of thirty-five eleven-year-olds. Mr Egerton the teacher was very patient but she felt a failure.

Towards the end of the teaching practice she went with the class on a week's field trip to Snowdonia. As they arrived in Llanberis on the first evening she felt shivery. She had an awful night and woke with a temperature. Mr Egerton said:

"As we are staying in a youth hostel we cannot leave you behind. Their rules include closing between ten am and five pm. I'm afraid you'll have to be at the back of the minibus. It's a great nuisance as I had been relying on you to take one of the small groups to look at rocks."

The rest of that week was a blur for her jolting about in the minibus. There was fog on Snowdon. Mr Egerton's looks got blacker as the week went on. In the second hostel at Bettys-Coed she dreamt:

"I was in a big bed with two men and two women. One of the men was Richard. I cheated and took my clothes off because I hoped for sex. The women were furious. Out of bed they poured water over me."

Despite everything she got her PGCE and became pre-occupied in looking for a job. She had had paid secondment to go to college. Now she was in the Re-deployment pool. She visualised this as a giant goldfish bowl. Head teachers looking for staff would put their nets in the bowl and trawl for good sound fish. She was finally fished out by the head of a small school in the northern Fens.

❖⟶⟜◉⟞⟵❖

"I don't understand why you are feeling so low."
Richard.

"You are not looking very well. Would you like a load of logs? It must be hard keeping warm in the cottage."
Pamela Hanchett.

"I'm going to prescribe you valium to help with your anxiety." *Her G.P.*

"Why did you buy a double bed?" *Her mother.*

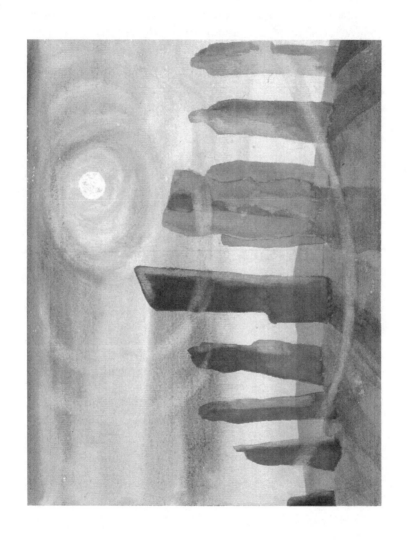

The Shadows

1977

When she started teaching, for real, after college, her life became dominated by the Fens. The Fens of Eastern England stretch from west Norfolk, through parts of Cambridgeshire and the Isle of Ely, into southern Lincolnshire. The Black Fens are situated inland from the Wash. As in Holland, the land has been reclaimed, over centuries from the sea and marshy swamps. It is irrigated by a vast complex of waterways. The land is as flat as the sea, stretching to the horizon and there are few trees or buildings to break the monotony. Some people wax lyrical about the beauty of the fens – the huge skies, the silence, the sense of endless space. For Ann who loved hills, the fens became in 1977 quite literally, soul destroying.

The school to which she has been appointed as a probationary teacher was, unhappily, called The Shadows. She had always been a sufferer from what is termed 'the pathetic fallacy'. She had a tendency to project her emotions onto the natural world. Perhaps it was, in part, a legacy from her maternal grandfather. Romantic painters created gloomy or exhilarating atmospheres in pictures of the Alps, gushing waterfalls and the Great Wilderness of America.

The bleak, black soil of the Fens expressed exactly how she felt and reflected back a sense of dejection and futility…

The head teacher had stressed how lucky she was to have been given her job. On the first morning when the children lined up by class in the playground, before going into the gloomy grey Victorian building, she watched the deputy head get the restless pupils into line. After the classes had gone in he said to her:

"Push 'em hard on the first day and you'll have much less trouble later. Watch it with the boys you'll be having for craft. Can't abide the subject myself; it's a complete waste of time and we've got very few materials anyway…got to economise…"

This was light years away from all the discussions in college about motivating children to learn, following their interests especially in teaching art, treating them with respect etc.

That Christmas term she got up early every morning and drove for an hour northwards, across a desolate landscape of frozen black fields, grey dykes and lowering skies. She passed the occasional small holding or farm. No one seemed to be about. Fierce dogs barked. In some fields the cabbages and Brussels sprouts stretched in lines to a vanishing point on the horizon. Telegraph poles along the roads became systematically smaller as they receded. It was a perfect model for a lesson in perspective drawing. What chilled her spirit was the rigid determinism, the ruthless logic of regression. In a landscape with hills perspective is defined by colour, darker near to, paler on the horizon. What was she doing in this landscape? Would she ever escape from it?

Two years ago going out to work had seemed like an option, not a grinding necessity. Now she had to survive as a teacher or go under. There was no one to rely on. No back up. She had to earn a sufficiency each month. How had she got herself into this situation?

The answer was clear and insistent. Because of 'love' you sinned. This is your hell, your punishment. You committed adultery, you fornicated, and this is the consequence. As she drove home, in the evening, exhausted, she wondered was he worth it? Was what she got from him in any way recompense? What was he anyway? Some kind of faery lover conjured out of summer meadows? She began to grow really angry and frustrated with herself.

"Show me your history project, Mrs Hales."

The education authority inspector for probationary teachers looked at the seven year old children's paintings of mediaeval castles displayed on the classroom walls. Their colourful pictures of Castle Rising, Castle Acre and Norwich were double mounted, as per the regulation, and looked attractive. Nice little bits of writing were similarly mounted. The children had enjoyed the topic and entered into it enthusiastically. She felt it showed the best of her teaching. Now this large fat man with red hair and a beard seemed keen to find fault and put her down.

"Not bad for a beginner, I suppose," he muttered. "But you are not in a special needs classroom now, Mrs Hales, we expect rather more in the primary sector."

So that was it. By leaving a special school she had added to the competition for posts among primary school teachers at a time of severe educational cut backs. He made her feel under valued and unwelcome in the profession. She knew they looked for excuses to make redundancies. However after a term she was still in post.

The Christmas holidays began. She spent rather a lot of time alone with a very large Christmas tree given her by a kind neighbour. She reflected sadly on earlier Christmas holidays – watching the front half of a donkey in a school nativity play, a gnome topple off his toadstool, Joseph stumble over his long robe. She had a second bout of flu.

On December 27th the people at the Merchants' House phoned to say they were giving a party on New Year's Eve, would she like to go? She was thrilled, but what could she wear. She decided that the dress she bought for a party in the Avenue, three years ago, would do. It was dark blue with a pattern of gold sequins round the collar.

Later that day she bumped into her neighbour from 4 Smith's Row. Alan was a retired lecturer, apparently on his own, and friendly.

"Are you going to the Merchants on New Year's Eve? They've just invited me as well. Shall we go together?"

Things, she felt were looking up, a party and a partner.

When they arrived at eight pm the party was in full swing. The beautiful old house was packed with people. There was dancing in a large drawing room and supper laid out in the dining room. Alan introduced her to people and she saw several she had already met – the vicar Hugh, Pamela from the hall, two of the doctors from the practice.

Alan was attentive without being overbearing. He was also a very good dancer. She was enjoying herself immensely when suddenly she saw Clare and Richard and their family standing in front of a mirror on the far side of the drawing room. She presumed Pamela had brought them along.

On the radio Big Ben chimed midnight, the small band played the opening bars of 'Auld Lang Syne', they crossed arms and she was crushed between Alan and another neighbour. Across the room Richard stooped and kissed his wife, their children gathered round them. She was swept by an icy sense of exclusion, of being, for ever, on the outside. She should have been with her own children.

❖⸱⸱▸═◉═◂⸱⸱❖

Winter, in the end, gave way to spring. Even the Fens improved with cow parsley to soften the hard edges and great skies of blue with cumulus clouds. By the start of the summer term of 1978 she was just beginning to feel slightly more confident. She enjoyed taking her pupils swimming and there were several school trips with mums coming along to help. At half term the next blow fell. Because of more education cuts the school had got to lose a teacher. Without consulting anyone she assumed the head was right when he said:

"I'm afraid it's a case of last one in has to be the first one out. But I'll have a word with Raymond I believe he needs someone…"

Raymond was the head of the other primary in the area, St Michael's, a larger, more modern school. Of course, she was grateful.

Raymond turned out to be a charmer and very good looking. He knew she was desperate for a job. He also knew that she had been misled by her head. She did not *have* to leave the Shadows but it suited him to have a grateful probationary teacher to replace a scale-2 teacher who was off indefinitely, suffering from stress. Mrs Hales would be pliant and a lot cheaper. She was also willing to coach the netball team and take them to matches on Saturdays.

The Christmas term saw the same dreary commuting through the sprout fields. She got up earlier and was home later. She had a larger, older class than at the Shadows. Teaching maths was again her Achilles Heel. Most Saturdays there was a netball match.

"It's great, Miss, we never won before..."

At the start of the Christmas holiday she met Hugh, the vicar, in the main street.

"You're looking tired, Ann. How goes it?"

To her great embarrassment she began to cry.

"Come back to the vicarage and we can talk."

She talked for an hour. It poured out. He was a sensitive listener. His long, thin face like an El Greco painting. She told him about feeling guilty, and about feeling punished. She missed her children and her marriage. She was fed up always waiting for Richard. Never knowing when he would come.

"It's very hard for some of us to live with uncertainty. That's what you have to do.

"I sometimes think I have strayed into someone else's life. This isn't mine. I don't really live in Hanchett. One day soon I'll wake up back in the Avenue – no adultery, a good Catholic, no separation, no fenland school…"

"Back to some earlier state of innocence…If only we could do that…"

Pastoral counselling was still in its early days. Hugh was very interested in it. Since the fifties Carl Roger's Client Centred Therapy had been gaining credence, particularly among forward looking churchmen. Its core conditions were acceptance, non-judgmental listening, reflecting back what the client said and offering unconditional love.

When she left she was surprised by the strength and length of his hug. His body felt tense and undernourished. She was grateful for being listened to so generously but she was also vaguely disquieted. She had realised in the last two years that there was something about her condition that aroused the interest of sympathetic men.

Her G.P. was a personable Welshman in his forties. He let her talk for ages on 'double' appointments, and steadily increased her valium. She began to fear losing her mental acuity. She slept like a log and awoke feeling sodden. It was getting increasingly hard to face the day. She smoked two king size cigarettes before she got up.

That Christmas she went home from school with a boxful of books. On Boxing Day, alone in the cottage, she got out some books with the intention of preparing maths lessons for the next term. She looked at the textbook. It made no sense at all. She started to shiver uncontrollably and an icy hand clutched her insides. She felt panic and despair. 'I cannot do this. I cannot go back next term'.

Her G.P. gave her two weeks sick leave for emotional stress and chronic fatigue. He gave her two more weeks and then two more. Just before half term Raymond came to see her.

"When are you coming back, Ann?"

"I don't know."

"It's half term next week, if you are not coming back after that, the fairest thing would be for you to resign."

February brought snow and very harsh weather. She slept for hours. She did less and less in the day except watch television on a small black and white set, open tins and drink Dubonnet. Sometimes at night she would walk up the lane and look back at her cottage with all its lights on. It was like a beacon. The one certainty left in her world.

As the evening went on she grew more cheerful than she had been all day at the prospect of sleep, oblivion, and a brief cessation of the daily struggle to live. She knew that her bed was the only really safe place in the world. In it she could for a while forget the pain that dragged her down all her waking hours. It was a sad disappointment as she awoke 'feeling light-hearted' to see the devil Misery sitting on her pillow waiting to walk with her throughout the day until the next night.

One day Richard appeared out of the snow.

"Haven't you got this teaching thing cracked yet? What's taking you so long?"

The next day she had a long talk to Mary who told her that their mother was unable to look after herself at home and was going to stay for a bit in a convent nursing home.

"It would be good if we could go and see her together."

"I don't think I can leave here. Yet".

An old friend from Oxford telephoned regularly and made her promise she would go and stay at Easter time. At present even going to the village shop or to see the G.P. was a big undertaking.

A thaw came and then a letter from the education authority. She was summoned to a meeting at Shire Hall. The officials repeated what Raymond had said:

"The fairest thing to do is to resign."

The inspector with red hair and a beard chipped in:

"I could see when I visited you at the Shadows you were struggling."

Not knowing what else to do she resigned... Then, in despair, she consulted her union. The man she saw got very angry on her account.

"Why ever didn't you come and see us earlier. You should never have resigned..."

trethevy Quoit '95   A Hales

204

Moving On

1979

"Somewhere in the heaven
Of lost futures
The lives we might have lived
Have found their own fulfilment."

Eavan Boland [1]

She sat in the car outside the employment exchange. She had reached the bottom of the deep pit down whose slippery side she had been sliding for months.

No job, no job prospects and no unemployment benefit. She does not remember driving back to the cottage.

Next day there was a letter telling her she had not got the post of assistant librarian at her old college. "We feel that although you are having a difficult patch, it would be a pity if you left the teaching profession at this stage."

There was a rare letter from Richard.

"More and more now, for reasons I cannot explain,

I shall be withdrawing from your life. If I don't a lot of people will get hurt."

She didn't know what he was talking about. She felt she had hardly got the energy to find out. Their relationship over the past five years had resembled a beach in Cornwall – rocks with a swirling tide of ebbs and flows. Several times she had tried to put an end to it. Several times he had disappeared for weeks. When he was in difficulties his dependency had seemed to increase. At those times she had loved him most. Success in people attracted him. Her misery and depression had helped to drive him away. Probably they were each looking for someone to fix them. Perhaps they were making each other worse?

A few weeks later he phoned one evening:

"Can you meet me in the Hanchett Arms, now?"

"Why there?"

"I've something to tell you."

This sounded ominous. Mystified and apprehensive she walked through a stormy night. After getting their drinks he lit up. He spoke gently, almost kindly:

"I told you, Ann, when we first met, that one day, not in a blaze of glory, but on an ordinary grey day, it would be over…"

She said nothing, but she thought; now it's not a grey day but a filthy black night. He lit another cigarette.

"You have to make your own way now…I have perhaps been able to help you with my little philosophies, but not any more…"

She stood up.

"Your greatest liability was in loving me" he said ruefully with a touch of tenderness.

She left the pub, stumbled back to the cottage, and threw a newly opened pack of cigarettes into the stove. In fact it took a long time to give up smoking completely.

She stayed up all night and wrote a long suicide note starting:

"I used to think that dying was a coward's way out… not any more. I used to think that suicide was the one unforgivable sin. Now I believe that is nonsense…" and on for three pages with messages for all her loved ones.

She never did anything with the letter because that morning the postman delivered twelve copies of her newly published book, *"The Children of Skylark Ward."* Almost at once the phone started to ring with messages of congratulation.

The deputy head of a local special school said he had been asked to review the book for a magazine. He very much liked the look of it – the white outline of a bird on a blue background.

"I like your quote from the Caged Skylark by Manley Hopkins…I don't know whether you'd be interested but we'll be interviewing shortly for a teacher. Would you consider applying?"

The urgency about ending her life receded. The depression was just beginning to budge although there was still a long way to go.

She got the job and with great difficulty began to reduce her dose of valium. Every reduction, however minute, was extraordinarily disorienting. On the first days after a reduction she felt completely out of touch with herself. She felt as if she saw herself from a long way off. She felt as if she had no feeling. It was all very odd and in a way the maddest she ever felt. This coming off process took her months. She decided she had an 'addictive personality'. She was addicted to valium, cigarettes and dangerous love. But she kept her job going.

During the summer holidays she took some young people on holiday to southern Spain. While they cavorted in the sea she wrote in her journal:

"I'm the woman whom God forgot. In the last four years I have passed from life to a living death. I am alone in a deep pool of loneliness. Many times, lately, I have tried to reach another human being, but as my fingers grasp theirs a strong current bears me away. Here in Spain I know I must make one more tremendous effort to reach out, or I shall perish."

They were in the foothills of the Sierra Apuljarra. The ancient Moorish village was scattered along the hillside and seemed bound to fall into the valley far below. The houses were square and white with thick tile roofs of a pinkish-brown. The hills above were sharp and conical covered in boulders and rocky screes. In contrast there were little strips of green. These were meadows that grew vines, tomatoes, beans and potatoes watered by streams fed from distant heights and channelled into Roman aqueducts. The contrast between the gaunt slopes and the radiant strips had spoken to her.

When she got home there was an invitation to a day conference run by 'Depressives Anonymous'. A speaker said:

"Sometimes a depressed person will put off what she knows to be an important decision. I invite you all, now, to consider in five minutes silence what that decision might be for you. Write it down and start acting on it tomorrow."

She seemed to know, at once, what her decision would be. She must leave Hanchett, move back into Cambridge, not to live with anyone but in her own small house and garden. Life in the country was not for her any more. Certainly not in the Fens.

She had done some work on the cottage in the past three years. There was a warm indoors bathroom, and a fully fitted kitchen extension. She put the cottage on the market and it sold immediately at more than double her original purchase price. Finding a house in Cambridge took much longer. Luckily her would be purchaser was prepared to wait. He waited nine months. She became despairing. Any house that was affordable, and that she liked, had some awful flaw. She was not surprised. At that time any small decision like buying a pair of shoes, or even what to have for supper, seemed difficult. Making up her mind about a house got harder and harder. A wise friend said:

"Don't give up hope. One of these days you will walk into a house and it will say to you 'I've been waiting for you.' And that will be the one."

She saw an advertisement for a house in Priory Road. She did not know the street but as she read, and re-read the advert, it all had a curiously familiar feel to it. She went to see it. She was surprised to find the street in an historical area off the Newmarket Road. She had not known of its existence… The terraced house was ordinary enough but as its owner let her out into a wilderness of back garden she was overcome with emotion. She knew that this was the garden she had always longed for. It was a secret garden; large for the size of the house and filled with overgrown rose bushes, lilac, flowers in profusion and a huge central pear tree.

In Hanchett she said good-bye to her friends.

Hugh said: "I hope you find someone in Cambridge if you feel like going on with counselling."

Alan said:" I'll miss you, Ann. You've been a good neighbour. Four years go quickly in village life."

The couple who kept the shop said: "Come back and see us sometimes."

The cottage remained in her dreams for the rest of her life. Every now and again she would be either going back

to live there, looking for the cottage, or trying to leave.
Someone wrote a book about House as image of the Self.
She felt the concept was borne out in her life.

---

[1] *New Collected Poems by Eavan Boland, Carcanet Press, 2005*

Priory Road

1980 Onwards

The area was historical, beneath the ground. Priory Road built in 1898 ran from the Abbey House down to the river. My house was end of terrace and looked towards a grassy mound with an old building known as the Cellarer's Chequer.

I began to meet my neighbours. Next door was an old lady who had been born in her house. Opposite there was an old gentleman who had been born in his. There were a lot of young families because it was designated a General Improvement Area and grants for rebuilding and modernising were available.

These young owners had worked together to improve their houses and there was a flourishing Priory Residents Association which used a small old building, at one side of my house. This had been named the Frater in recognition of the fact that all the buildings in the area stood on the site of a mediaeval priory. Frater would have been the name used for the monks' refectory. Later I discovered that my garden probably grew over what had been the monks' herbarium.

I delved into the history of this area called Barnwell. Apparently it was once Barnwelle, a place of fresh, pure springs. The name meant Children's Wells. The children were the young people who wrestled and played games here to celebrate the midsummer. Pre-Christian revels were often turned later into celebrations of the Birthday of St John the Baptist on June 24th. So was this always an ancient sacred place?

In 1092 a priory was founded in Cambridge by the Canons Regular following the rule of St Augustine. This was at the foot of Castle Hill. In 1112 the monastery was re-founded to the east of Cambridge in the Barnwell area. Here was the great open space called Barnwell Field, not enclosed until the 18th century. The new priory was midway between Midsummer Common and Stourbridge Common. These areas of common land had fairs granted to the town by King John in 1211. The monks of Barnwell were granted the considerable dues from the Midsummer Fair which was frequented by pilgrims on their way to the shrine of St Ethelburgha at Ely. Our word tawdry comes from the shoddy quality of some things sold at the fair as offerings to be taken on to the shrine of St Audrey. Dues from what became the great international fair at Stourbridge went to the Leper hospital further east in Barnwell Field.

As I wandered round my new area I looked up the hill that rises from the river towards the higher terraced ground. I imagined the great Priory Church with its tower and the monastic buildings stretched along the top of the ridge bordering what is now the busy Newmarket road. This was once a Roman road to Norwich.

I thought about Nicholas Smith, the prior who was obliged to resign in 1534 to make way for the Dissolution. Had he struggled to secure a better fate for his priory? What did the local people feel about the threatened loss of their monastery?

"Nicholas skirted the abbey, passing round the Lady Chapel at the east end of the church. He breathed a silent prayer as he looked up at the lancet windows. 'Mother of God, please help me make the right decisions. Look down on your abbey and keep us safe.'"

Whatever he prayed, Nicholas was succeeded by John Badcock appointed by Royal Warrant to supervise the Dissolution. The commissioners for the Dissolution were the notorious Dr Legh and William Cavendish. They arrived in November 1538 and received a deed of surrender signed by the prior and six canons. "They took an inventory of movable and removable objects and some cattle" [1]. A number of tiles were taken, so the buildings were left roofless, no doubt hastening their ruin. Stones were carted away and used in college building. It is thought that the chequer building somehow kept its roof and was then used as a stable.

In 1550 the priory and its lands were granted to Sir Anthony Browne who was physician to Henry VIII. It had been a substantial priory with land in Chesterton and Cambridge.

I was relieved that it had not been Sir William Petre who had been the commissioner for this dissolution although he acquired manors in Cambridgeshire among his many acquisitions at this time [2]. I had absorbed the idea, from my Petre grandmother, that Sir William was a good and honourable catholic. When I looked into the records it seems he did not act cruelly at any of the religious houses that he was in charge of dissolving, mostly in the West Country, but he purchased, at this time, many of the dissolved properties. At the least he was a very shrewd man who avoided any situation in which he had to choose between loyalty to his faith and to his sovereign.

At night I looked at the Abbey House built in 1678 on the site of the monastery. The house was lived in by council tenants and looked very run down. The walled garden was a jungle. The full moon rose between its towering chimneys and cast great blue shadows over the roofs.

Over the years I wondered about the bad things that happened occasionally in the area, like a violent death or the greed of a property developer. Was it fanciful to see a connection between these things and the dark past of the area? Can the history of a house influence its present inhabitants?

Stories and pictures of the area wove themselves into my dreams. One night I dreamt I was a crocus in my garden with a very long root. A man came and tried to yank me out of the ground. I woke screaming "Leave me be...Leave me here..."

The locality wrought changes in me. For the first time in my life I began to write poetry and to paint. I also began to record my dreams. Walking in the evening by the river the moon rose and the sun set across Midsummer Common with colleges and churches silhouetted against a changing sky.

Priory Road, like Nancledra years before in Cornwall,

afforded me a place of sheltered habitation. I began to stabilise. I grew more confident at work and began to take training courses that addressed the growing awareness that people with special needs could use therapeutic skills in addition to just physical care. Valerie Sinason at the Tavistock clinic started to pioneer work in which very handicapped people were asked what they were feeling and what they wanted. I eventually got secondment to go on her courses and then to start a simple kind of counselling for some of the children in school.

I had been back in Cambridge about two years when Mary telephoned.

"She's much worse. Can you come?"

I got two days unpaid leave and went to Surrey.

"Mum. It's alright, we're here, we'll look after you."

She looked terrified with no speech. What had happened to her? She didn't seem to recognise us. She was like a stricken deer. The nuns said she had had a series of strokes and fallen heavily. They said she did not have very long. She was seventy-nine. She had been a widow and had lived alone for twenty-seven years.

"I'll stay, Ann, you should get back to your job".

I was very reluctant to leave. I went to sit with my mother before I went home. Her eyes were closed. She seemed to be sleeping. I got up to go. At the door I paused and looked back. Her eyes were open, she was looking at me, and then, slowly, she raised her arm. I have wondered about that ever since. Was she waving good bye or asking me to stay?

After two days Mary phoned. She told me our mum had had another stroke and died at once. No one was with her. An intuition had warned me to stay and I had ignored its voice.

I went to see her lying in the convent chapel. Now she looked serene and like the photographs on her wedding day when she was twenty-three. There was a childlike innocence about her, as if she was unsoiled by this world's trafficking. What was immature and undeveloped in her had, in her final look, an appeal of its own. The separations and losses she had suffered as a child shaped her quality of mothering. She always remained shy and unassertive. In every part of her life and her being she missed her William. But she had always been there for me. Deeply distressed as she had been at the breakdown of my marriage, she had remained loving and supportive. Now she was gone and I was filled with regrets. I had been to see her so little during the Hanchett years.

We buried her in a cemetery surrounded by trees in the North Downs, near where she had lived since she had left Essex. After her death her older sister in South Africa consulted a medium who said:

"Your sister has been very afraid of dying...but now she is at peace."

Helen was ill in California and unable to get to the funeral.

Five months later Mary phoned:

"Not good news from Helen, darling."

Helen's husband had telephoned to say she had been

treated for a rare leukaemia. It had been in remission for a while but had now returned. Helen had not told us this earlier because she had not wanted to upset our mother.

"He wants one of us to go at once. What do you think?"

I knew I wanted to go, very much.

"I could go… Provided they'll give me unpaid leave… the money would be a bit of a problem…"

She sounded relieved.

"Don't worry we'll find some funds from our mother's estate to cover the air fare and your loss of income".

Mary saw me off at Heathrow. Although I was going alone I felt she was with me. As sisters we were united.

Watching the clouds below the plane, stretching like an endless snowfield, under the piercing blue sky, I marvelled at how easy leaving home had been. Two years ago a walk to the shops in Hanchett had been an ordeal.

I flew the polar route to San Francisco. It was a very long day and in the sunlight I felt transfixed by an everlasting blueness. I hung above the world and all the time something terrible was happening to my sister. Her husband had said to Mary:

"Do come…she has a fifty-fifty chance".

Later I wrote:

"Throughout this long, long day
I have been cloaked in blue,

219

Off Greenland's coruscated shore
Water shivered black and gold.
Circling over Baffin Bay
Rents in the cotton showed
Unseen sea – cathedral floor
Pitted with votive candle shards

Throughout this Icarus day
I have been dazed by blue
Falling over Hudson's Bay
As far as eye could reach
Lakes of purple, copper, violet, rose,
Set in the sand
Beside a turquoise sea.

At the end of this spectrum day
All colours spin,
'You've come before my long, long night'."

Helen's friends met me at the airport and we went for a meal before going to the hospital. Helen looked thin and wasted but her cheeks were puffy from the treatment. Her red gold hair steamed across the pillow. Her deep husky voice was the same.

"Will you look after P.? It's such a shame I have to be in here while you are visiting."

I had never visited her in America and she had gone to live there in the 1960s.

"I'll make him lots of puddings! I'll be back tomorrow when we can talk more".

I slept late in the friends' cool ranch house. They dropped me off at the hospital. Helen had a room on her own. No one was about so I went in and sat beside her. She seemed to be in a deep sleep. Time passed. P. arrived. He looked at her.

"I think we should call a nurse".

They came and put us out of her room. There was a flurry of activity with staff appearing from all directions and a doctor giving orders. We sat silent and tense in the waiting area. After an hour the doctor came to speak to us.

"We are afraid she has haemorrhaged into her brain."

From a long way away I heard my voice asking:

"Is she terminally ill?"

"I'm afraid so…"

"How long?" asked P.

"Probably a few hours

Jet lag and shock made it all seem unbelievable.

"I had no idea that she was this ill."

"No one knew. That's Helen. Kept everything to herself if it was bad news."

He started to weep.

"Would you like to be with her now?" a nurse asked.

I remember the rest of that long day in a cool room. The blinds were drawn and the walls were green. It was like being underwater. At some point a priest came to anoint her. About twenty to eight in the evening P. was stroking her hands and suddenly the heart monitor surged briefly and then the bleep failed. Helen had said good bye and gone.

She had been sixteen when our father had died, in more or less the same way of a brain haemorrhage. She was forty-three and childless.

I had a lot of time to think about her life on the flight home. I was thirteen when she was born and I had doted on her. I think I felt she was my baby. She was always beautiful with her red gold hair and green eyes.

We wondered about a cause for her leukaemia. A friend from Oxford told me that a piece of research had suggested that the enthusiasm for x-raying the foetus in utero in the thirties might have caused cancer when such people were about thirty. It turned out that Helen and a school friend both started to be ill in their thirties. It is quite possible that our mother was x-rayed more than once when she was pregnant in 1938–39.

The night after I returned from America to Priory Road I dreamt:

"I am driving R down Pall Mall, but it's also a country road with a ragged grass strip in the middle. R is sitting in the back. He has difficulties with his sight. We pass mounted soldiers on manoeuvres. He is excited and shouts that it's the best he's seen so far. The soldiers gallop on our left, behind a thin hedge, towards a castle.

I am deeply satisfied that I am giving him this opportunity to see. It's as if I am giving him sexual pleasure.

After a while he says:' it's like a black shutter coming down.' As he is speaking I am experiencing the shutter myself. He's disappointed and I try to console him. I am suffused with tenderness for him that has little to do with the sexual clamour that fills my head."

Later I interpreted all that as being about blindness and not being able to see what was really going on in my life. My sexuality had obscured the truth of other things. Deterioration of my actual eyesight became a metaphor for the state of my psyche.

---

[1] *The Observances in Use at the Augustinian Priory of St Giles and St Andrew at Barnwell, Cambridge, 1897*

The Inheritors of Barnwell Priory, P.V.Danckwerts, Proceedings of the Antiquarian Society, 1981

[2] *Tudor Secretary, E.G.Emmison, Longmans, 1961*

Eyesight

1983

Ihadn't heard from him for years and there he was on the phone.

"I've got two places in the choir stalls from my friend at King's for Ash Wednesday Evensong. Would you like to come? Meet you outside the chapel door at five-fifteen."

I had often, in the past, dreamt about him before he put in an appearance. Now it had happened again. What was the implication of the 'eyesight' dream?

Did my unconscious evoke him? Was the dream some kind of warning? Perhaps there were intersections on some giant cobweb where we would always meet. He had once said:

"I don't want to be in your dreams."

It was an icy evening in February. The wind blew into Cambridge straight across the Wash from the Urals. The chapel stalls were comfortingly warm. Perched high above the choir in the richly carved stalls we were invisible. It felt as if we were suspended in glorious isolation from the rest of the world, lapped in the most glorious sound.

In the Allegri Miserere the treble boys' voices climb to the fan vaulting, pause in mid-air and then fall like seed pearls. It happens a number of times in the psalm – the running climb, the pause, the ecstatic shiver as the sound reaches a peak and curls over. During the singing it is as if there was no before, no after, just the now.

We had a glass of Madeira in the Crossed Keys before he hurried off home.

Seeing him had, of course, set off all the old longing. I went home and thought about Ash Wednesday – going to King's with my mother in 1949 – the familiar bitter-sweet of Lent – the denial, the abstinence, the intractability of a cold East wind.

The next day I was sitting in a staff meeting when I noticed I wasn't seeing properly. I closed my left eye, the right one was as usual. I closed my right eye and all I saw was a grey mist. Next day I woke and it was the same. I felt panicky and went to see my G.P. – another Scot – but not one keen to prescribe anti-depressants. He gave me a speedy referral to the eye consultant.

"It's probably a detached retina. You must rest for two weeks and come back. I shall then decide whether I need to operate."

I spent the fortnight painting and saying good bye to seeing things, I feared the worst.

"It's a very successful operation normally. I shall plug the small rent in your retina with sponge. Why did it happen? We don't really know why retinas detach – tear. It's more likely to happen to short sighted people as their retinas are a little more stretched."

While I was recovering consciousness I dreamt:

"I am inside the body of a multiply handicapped person. My body is lying on its side between two boards. Each part of my body is disjoined from the whole body, only one part can be mobilised at a time. It's like being a puppet. By pulling all the strings at once you get the body going."

The ward was old fashioned and friendly. Any injury to sight seems to evoke a lot of sympathy. I felt carried on a wave of kindness and concern.

My eyesight recovered completely.

The good friend, who had given me advice about finding a house 'speaking' to me, said:

"I wonder whether you have mourned sufficiently. You've had so many losses."

It was a good question. All those unshed tears stacked up and pressing from behind my eyes. Tears for the loss of my old married life, the deaths of my mother and Helen. There were the many losings of Richard. There had been a loss of job and professional status.

Seeing Richard lately, at King's, had made me realise that we would never be a couple. Perhaps that had always been a myth.

What was I going to do about the need to mourn? In the old Roman Missal that disappeared at the Council of Vatican

Two, there had been an ancient prayer 'For the Gift of Tears'. It is a gift. I had always envied those who could melt into tears easily. Sometimes I felt like the Ice Queen in the Hans Anderson fairy tale, with an ice splinter in my heart. Perhaps I should pay more attention to my dreams and write them down. Could someone tell me what they mean?

I went to some kind of group therapy and felt the facilitator was a very unusual man. He seemed to be spontaneous and unconventional. People in the group were fond of him. He was kindly and I responded to this.

Then I got shingles. My head said:

"You've got to do something about yourself. Your mother dies and then your sister, your retina detaches and now you've got shingles…Perhaps your body is telling you something."

It was some time later that I remembered the group conductor, who I'll call Merlin. I got in touch with him and we arranged to meet. I was somewhat daunted when he said:

"Come at exactly three o'clock. If you come any earlier I shall not answer the door."

So for the next three years at three o'clock, on two afternoons a week, I went to see him.

The night before our first meeting I dreamt:

"Looking out at tree top height across a spring wood. Down below a sale is going on beside a stream. There are fair booths and stacks of clean white pillowcases on the muddy river bank. Some of them are getting dirty".

I told the magician this dream and he said:

"Do you think you may be afraid that things belonging to you will get spoiled by coming here?"

He had tapped into my feelings of apprehension. What am I doing, I had asked myself. Will I make my life harder by talking about the painful things? Am I opening a can of worms? What did the clean white pillowcases symbolise? Was there a danger that I would totally collapse and go completely mad?

We talked for the agreed fifty minutes and I drove home feeling much lighter. I felt I wanted to dance across the unfolding sunset sky, hand in hand with the magician.

That night Richard telephoned to ask if he could come over. I did not want him to come but I couldn't say 'No'.

On my next visit to Merlin I told him about Richard.

"Is he going to become your life-partner?"

"No"

"Then you must stop seeing him."

Neg. 06-Jul, Midsummer   A.B.

Dreams

Merlin believed that everyone and everything, in any dream, was part of the dreamer. So if I dreamt about a builder, or a doctor, or a burglar, for example, this person might be a stand in for Merlin, but only in so far as there was a Merlin-aspect of myself. My dreams often cast a man in a position of authority. Merlin would see that as the male part of me. I would see it as Merlin and behind him, my father, and behind him either the Church or God.

Merlin soon showed me how each dream is awash with symbolic riches. These treasures are available if the dreamer observes and meditates on the dream's content. I had kept a dream journal since I came to Priory Road. The more I recorded dreams the more vivid and accessible they became. Merlin's interest in my dreams brought on a veritable explosion. Sometimes I remembered three dreams when I awoke. I got used to writing them down on waking as daylight soon seemed to remove their initial gloss. It was easy to mis-remember if a few daylight hours had passed. At the height of therapy I would even tape the dream if I woke in the night. My voice in the following dream was eerily sepulchral. When I spoke on tape at four am I was still very shaken by the dream.

"I go down into a semi-basement room. There's a man

down there and he's zipping things up in a black bag. He does not hide the fact that he is a burglar. He says 'That's fine…they'll be back tomorrow for the furniture"

His clothes are expensive. He has the devil's face. I go upstairs and look in the rooms, …all the pictures have gone. I start weeping really loudly…I want to be comforted…' all the pictures have gone; all the pictures have gone, nothing's left…everything is gone'. I cry so loudly that I wake up crying and shouting."

I still feared that the process of therapy would rob me of something very precious. I feared at times that I would lose my religious faith, that Merlin might become my only god.

In therapy I was seeking some kind of break from the imprisonment of my self and of my past. Merlin felt that the aim of therapy was to enable a person become a freer spirit. I had a very long way to go and it was all hard, painful work. Merlin seemed to remain always optimistic about a good outcome.

In my third year with him, in the February, I dreamt:

"I am negotiating a high narrow bridge across the river Chet. It's been constructed high in the air following the line of the actual bridge."

This is the bridge that forms the boundary of the Langley estate. On the Langley side is the village of Chedgrave; on the other side is the larger village of Loddon.

"*I want to cross from the Langley side. I have almost crossed, but the bridge is extremely unsafe because it is just made of baskets piled together. At each step they part and give way. I am in a dilemma. If I go back to get help I may never get this far again. Once or twice I try a tentative step. The whole structure seems likely to collapse. Suddenly I make some kind of act of faith, or total commitment, or total self-abandonment, and, as if by magic, I am over on the other side.*"

In finally crossing this precarious bridge I think I was making a break with my past.

For us, as children, crossing the bridge led to a wider world. The baskets were like the dilly bags made by the Maori. An expression, no doubt, of the feminine side of myself.

A second dream that night was again set by the Chet Bridge, on the Langley side.

"*An armadillo has bitten a man. I see him dying in a most horrendous way.*

His body, in a series of bloody explosions, has pushed his head through his anus. I watch his bloodied, plump face on the last stage of its journey, being pushed out. Nothing of the rest of his body remains. It's been blown to bloody bits and lies about the place.

I watch this remarkable scene with a feeling of utter detachment. I feel neither pity nor revulsion, just amazement"

I suppose this curious birth-death dream is a symbolic exploding of the tie between my self and my father. It wasn't my father's face in the dream but the shape of it was his, and it felt like being about him. Perhaps a distorted male part of myself was being blown away to make room for a more moderate maleness.

There were many dreams in which I was extraordinarily passive or even servile. Having precious things stolen from me without resistance, people torturing me for no good reason.

> *"I'm witnessing terrible cruelties... In one scene, men like S.S. Officers are operating on a young woman's stomach and she is saying, in extreme self-abasement,' I'll breathe as little as possible' – as if to draw breath is a privilege to which she is not entitled?"*

In therapy I very gradually came to see that I could make even a stroppy taxi-driver into some kind of authority figure. But 'seeing' it was not enough to change a lifelong habit of obeisance to authority, male or female.

It was very hard to get hold of my mother in the therapy sessions. My father always seemed to fill the room. I had the sensation of her slipping out as I came in, or she presented in dreams as a veiled figure, or a faceless woman. It was hard to be critical about any of her actions, I always wanted to defend and protect her. I am so closely identified with her spirit, that at times, it is her feeling of being 'an unwanted woman' or 'a woman of no consequence' that then becomes my feeling too. I dreamt:

"I met a woman long since dead walking very very slowly back from church. She was looking down on the ground. She had fine clothes – a very long skirt of black silk and a grey silk shirt and jacket. A veil completely covered her head and face. She didn't see me. I passed and then she turned, lifted her head and smiled. I think I was not going to speak to her, just pass her by, but I changed my mind and greeted her. I was surprised by the warmth and gentleness of her smile. She seemed happy."

Sometimes, as in the dream at the start of the chapter on Acton Burnell, I *am* my mother. That dream happened on the night of her birth date, September 27th. It is Marjorie on the roof of her home struggling to cope with her three daughters.

To have empathy for others, to be able to stand in their shoes and see the world as they do, comes with a price. I do not always want to see the world through my parents' eyes. I had to learn that Merlin was entirely his own self.

In my dreams Merlin turned up wearing many different disguises. He might be a burglar, a builder, or a brain surgeon. He was a very large man and his nurturing quality could be experienced by me as maternal. Many people looked to him for succour. A dream I cherish went like this:

"A lot of us are going by coach to the sea. We got out on the beach and the coach threw itself down, on its side, sort of weary and fed up with all the driving, grumpy.

The spirit was glad to escape. As the spirit came out the coach was a nursing sow and all along its great belly there was bleeding, but it wasn't excessive – like ragged edges of flesh."

In my Norfolk childhood I remembered how a great nursing sow threw herself down against the edge of her sty and all the little piglets pushed and shoved to get a place to feed. She grunted with exhaustion and sometimes annoyance, but she remained available, for a while, to their hungry, thrusting, searching snouts. My mother once told me that while she and William were at a dinner party, the maid between each course said "three more, Sir" or "another five, Madam". Their prize sow was having her first litter. By the end of the evening she had had twenty-one piglets.

So Therapy dreams could be suffused with humour or intense joy:

"I am with a group of people in New York. Someone has given me a small vase to stand on my desk. It has white blossom growing out of it. I am surprised by joy."

It was such a wonderful feeling of undiluted joy. In memory I feel it still.

Merlin introduced me to the idea of an 'Atlas Personality'. This is a way of being sometimes shown by a person, who from early childhood has felt a particular responsibility for either, or both parents, and her siblings. An eldest child, a youngest child, an only child can all feel that burden of responsibility. Many of the world's carers may have started out as atlas children.

Atlas in Greek mythology was doomed to hold up the heavens, and have the whole globe of earth on his shoulders. The person who says of himself:

"Sometimes I feel responsible for the whole damn lot of them" is describing an atlas feeling. If anything goes wrong that person may feel particularly guilty.

I divided my sessions with Merlin between talking to him face to face, and lying on his sofa and expressing a chain of associated ideas, or images. One day lying on his sofa, I recounted the following 'day dream':

"I see Langley Hall Farm…beside the house the ground collapses into an underground cavern…I'm looking inside and it's familiar…I'm at the mouth of the cave and the sea is about waist height. It's very cool but a shaft of sun comes through a hole in the cave roof. The colour in the cavern is a very rich plum colour…coming towards me, fairly undefined, is a child with a globe on her back. She's bent by the weight of it…It's an atlas, a sphere of the world with the countries marked on it and now there's a ray of sunlight hitting…Africa…and now the child who was holding it has gradually crumbled and the sphere is floating away on the current…"

When I got home I painted what I had seen. As I was doing this I wondered 'why Africa?' Suddenly I remembered my mother's diary for 1931 and her holiday in Morocco. The sunbeam had certainly lit up that part of Africa.

Gradually I began to recover the feelings I had as a four year old when our parents had gone away and Mary and

I were taken to Acton Burnell. As I pondered on the scene –Merlin called it meditating– it seemed as if understanding those painful feelings gradually released a burden and the heavy globe became a balloon and drifted off on the current. It was not only separation from Mummy that had caused pain, it was also the feeling of 'being left behind' and a sense of responsibility for me and for Mary. Would we be looked after properly in her absence? Small wonder I looked peeky on her return.

During our third year I began to feel an end might be in sight. We talked about this. Finally we fixed it for December 16th. The last few months became countdown time. Each of our last eight meetings was a milestone and all the time December 16th loomed. I wept between sessions, but rarely in them. Once he said:

"I don't know why you weep. I should have thought ending would be something of a relief." He said this with genuine surprise, not unkindly.

On the night of December 15th I dreamt:

"G. (a son aged about 4 in the dream) has had to wait 3 hours before I pick him up from nursery school. The school closed at 1 pm and now it's 4 pm. He's nowhere to be found. I start to look for him in the surrounding streets and call his name. I look out across a great grey landscape of fields and marshes. In the middle distance by a hedge there's a movement. Can it be him? There's a terrible feeling of cruelty to G and his agony of mind, being thus abandoned by me."

I was overwhelmed by the sense of approaching loss which felt like a planned death. Once we had ended I knew I'd never see again the Merlin of our sessions. The man would remain but Merlin –all the people he had been for me– would be gone for ever, except, of course, in my dreams.

One day Merlin said, speaking with a slow grandeur:

"A sad Tale's best for Winter…Aloneness is never not here…and when one is with it…it is an existential reality that most of the time…at least in the West…we obfuscate, deny and alienate ourselves from…."

In one of my last dreams before December 16th I dreamt:

"I was standing on the seashore looking out to sea. Suddenly there was a great fish beside me, and then it was moving, slithering its huge bulk down the sand and into the sea. Then it was gone."

At our last meeting I told this dream to Merlin. He listened gravely and nodded: "Yes, I'll settle for that."

I walked out of his house for the last time. A half moon hung above the town. The rest of my life lay before me.

Journey through Solitude

" **A** loneness is never not here" Merlin had said, using one of his characteristic double negatives.

When I left my marriage thirty years ago I was starting a journey into aloneness – although I did not know this at that time. If I had known what such a journey involved would I have acted differently? I do not know.

Thirty years is roughly eleven thousand days, or about a quarter of a million hours. My mother lived alone for twenty-seven years. On a day when I have spoken to no one, is that a wasted day? A hermit or an anchoress would not think so.

One of the hardest things about living alone, I find, is the number of decisions that must be made; so much action that is solely self-motivated. The freedom of choice is at times overwhelming. Sometimes I listen to the voices talking inside my head.

"What are today's priorities? Make a list. Look at the time; if you are going to church you must get on with it.

I've got the hump and I don't know why. Get out into the garden… Must get some peanuts for the birds. There's a lovely breeze shall I do the washing today?"

I came into a solitary way of living quite suddenly. On the long journey down to Cornwall in 1976 I started to have intimations of what the future might hold… From being the cherished, though over worked, centre of a busy household, I became just me. The raison d'etre of my life had gone. Perhaps I under estimated the satisfaction I had felt in being over extended. For years I had had far too much to do, after the sojourn in Nancledra, I didn't have enough.

The suddenly bereaved man or woman has solitude thrust upon them. I had more choice about entering into the single state, so I felt a responsibility about creating the consequences of solitude.

"It's your own fault if you don't like it" said judgemental Ann, countless times, during the dreary Hanchett days. Nowadays I hear that voice less often…

Living alone is an art with many components.

Down the years I have gradually come to see myself as a worthwhile person. Through therapy, both given and received, I know myself to be a lovable person and one who can say "No!" without fearing the forfeiture of my own or someone else's esteem

More and more the journey into solitude has been a journey into greater loving, although I only came to see this lately.

In the end, it seems, loving and losing Richard, Merlin, my parents, my sister, my husband, and so many others, has brought immeasurable gains as well. Love and sorrow can widen the heart All the time the view looking backward changes. Happenings that seemed about abject failure and loss can now be seen as some kind of triumph. Hard won painful experience can lead into empathy.

Has my relationship with God changed since those early days in the Norfolk wood? At convent school and later in the Crucible I became very aware of the personality of Christ. I learnt about prayer and meditation. In the dreadful middle years I lost awareness of the presence of God in my life. I felt He had forgotten me. I felt abandoned and life was flavourless. Coming to live in Priory Road led to a re-igniting of my faith. The neighbourhood and my garden, the monks' herbarium, gradually worked some kind of healing. Nowadays God seems to be the same as the God of my childhood, a loving, supporting presence. One whom I could not live without.

His guises are numberless, from the ardent bridegroom of the Song of Songs, to the indefatigable Hound of Heaven. I fled Him down the nights and down the days and down the arches of the years. In mist of tears I hid from Him and under running laughter. But, in the end:

"Fear wist not to evade as Love wist to pursue". [1]

My old home in Norfolk has been so much more than a well-loved environment. The house and garden, the woods and fields are all still there. On returning I may recognise a clump of grass by a ditch exactly as it was in my childhood. A tree has grown larger and older but it's still the same tree as I sat under as a child. Such physical continuity is immensely consoling. The views of the Langley and Hardley marshes are the ones that my mother saw on her walks. The line of poplars that reminded her of a Monet painting are there, so is Hardley Church and the mysterious Manor.

Smells remain the same. I may catch a scent of the spring woods and suddenly 'see' Mary and me cantering along a grassy ride on the ponies, jumping the small fences she has laid across the path. I open a gate and its latch fits my fingers as if they have their own memory, and it creaks as it always did.

I drive along the road to Bungay. From my early bike rides I know each bend and small incline. In the Catholic church I look up to a crucifixion window above the altar. On either side of the cross hang the two thieves. The good one is calm and leans towards the Lord, the other in a dark green loincloth writhes and turns away. The angel in front of the good thief has a shining white robe. The one in front of the bad thief has a grubby grey dress. This difference impressed me as a child.

Merlin got quite excited when I told him about this clear separation of the good from the bad. I do not remember exploring with him, on that occasion, the 'depressive' or balancing position which Jesus held, hung between the two extremes.

Here in Bungay with my father buried in the graveyard I think about my own death. I could share his grave but feel I would be intruding! I prefer the idea of a field where the three counties of Cambridge, Essex and Suffolk meet and skylarks rise from the yellow flowers of oilseed rape... That will be a new kind of solitude.

---

[1] *The Hound of Heaven by Francis Thompson,*
Burns Oates & Washbourne Ltd, 1893.

Table of descent of William Petre and his children from 11th lord Petre

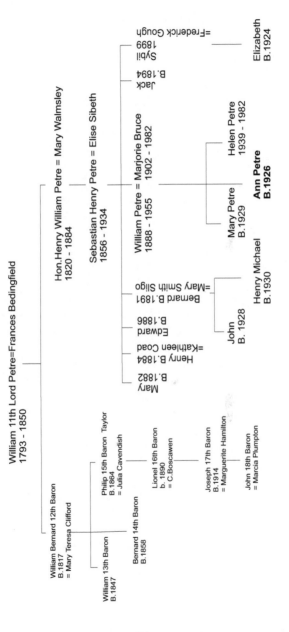

William 11th Lord Petre=Frances Bedingfield
1793 - 1850

Hon.Henry William Petre = Mary Walmsley
1820 - 1884

Sebastian Henry Petre = Elise Sibeth
1856 - 1934

Jack
B.1894

Sybil
1899
=Frederick Gough

Elizabeth
B.1924

William Petre = Marjorie Bruce
1888 - 1955   1902 - 1982

Mary Petre
B.1929

Ann Petre
B.1926

Helen Petre
1939 - 1982

Mary
B.1882

Henry B.1884
=Kathleen Coad

Edward
B.1886

Bernard B.1891
=Mary Smith Sligo

John
B. 1928

Henry Michael
B.1930

William Bernard 12th Baron
B.1817
= Mary Teresa Clifford

William 13th Baron
B.1847

Philip 15th Baron Taylor
B.1864
= Julia Cavendish

Bernard 14th Baron
B.1858

Lionel 16th Baron
b. 1890
= C.Boscawen

Joseph 17th Baron
B.1914
= Marguerite Hamilton

John 18th Baron
= Marcia Plumpton

Acknowledgements

I'd like to express great gratitude to my son, Hugh Hales-Tooke, for the use of the cover photograph, and to Ben and Anne Blower, the owners of North Cove Hall garden, where it was taken.

I thank the Penguin Group for permission to use the quotation from John Donne's poem 'A Nocturnal upon S. Lucy's Day'. The extract from 'The Sacred and Profane Love Machine', published by Chatto and Windus is reprinted by kind permission of The Random House Group Ltd. The Cambridge Evening News gave permission to use the photograph of the Governors of Addenbrookes Hospital taken in May 1970, and Hilary Ritchie, the Hospital Archivist, was very helpful in identifying the Governors.

I am grateful to my sister, Mary Pardoe and my cousin Elizabeth Edwards for supplying family photographs, and to Hugh for his work in preparing them for publication. My sincere thanks to Teresa Benison, my creative writing tutor, for her consistent encouragement and to Chris Thomas of Milton Contact Ltd for his editorial skills and great patience. Very special thanks to Jean Clark and Monique Viner for their detailed assessments of the text. Finally, gratitude to my sons Jonathan, Hugh and Giles for their constant support and very varied contributions to my life and to the book.

ISBN 1-905597-04-5

90000>

9 781905 597048